Cue Ball Christianity

Jeff Arias

Printed in the United States of America by Illumination Publishers.

ISBN: 978-0-9839157-7-5

Unless otherwise indicated, all Scripture references are from the Holy Bible, New International Version, copyright 1973, 1978, 1984 by the International Bible Society. Used by permission of Zondervan Bible Publishers.

About the author: Jeff Arias is a successful businessman who brings the faith of great men and women of the Bible into our modern life. He chalks out the way for powerful living in a challenging world. He is the husband of a beautiful Latina wife, Alex, and the father of four children. They reside in southern California. Jeff can be reached at jarias714@gmail.com.

Theatron Press
an imprint of Illumination Publishers

www.ipibooks.com
6010 Pinecreek Ridge Court
Spring, Texas 77379-2513, USA

Contents

To my wonderful wife Alex,
you have been a true champion at my side
enduring with me through thick and thin,
the highs and lows.
I love you with all my heart!

Acknowledgments

My sincere thanks to Elizabeth Thompson for your discipline and professionalism in editing this work. You have made my adventure in writing this book significantly less intimidating. Without your help this would still be on my life's to-do list. I wish you nothing but the very best in all your writing efforts.

Thank you to my friend Phil Garrison, who offered very early encouragement to continue with this venture, and was there along the way to help see me through.

Thanks to my two sisters, Liz and Tina. Liz, you offered me unbridled encouragement after reading some of my earlier writing, and Tina, you are one of the most talented artists I know. Thank you for your initial sketches for the cover.

Thank you to Steve Johnson, who offered to read my early manuscript and did, but then gave me constructive criticism in our phone conversation together.

To my friends in Hong Kong, Philip and Pandora Lam, thank you! You not only made our time in Hong Kong a pleasant one, but you helped to channel my energies for writing while living there. Also, to my friend Jim Heese, although you don't live in Hong Kong, I feel that our friendship is forever embedded in that wonderful city.

Thank you to my Thursday night Small Group Bible Study. The meeting we had one night where we discussed "getting out of the boat" helped me put teeth into getting this thing done. I wish you all nothing but success in all your endeavors.

To Bonnie Thompson who did an amazing job on the cover at the eleventh hour. Thank you!

Robert Carrillo, thank you for your friendship throughout the years. You have seen me at my best and my worst and have remained a pillar of support in my life.

To Manny and Nancy Arias, from the bottom of my heart, you are two of the best parents a kid could ever wish for. You have been a rock of support all my life and you could never be told thank you and I love you enough.

Finally, no work could ever be successful without the support of those closest to home. Thank you to my wife, Alex, and our four children. I feel blessed beyond words to have such a wonderful family. If no one else were to ever read this book beside you guys, then I would consider it a huge success. Thank you!

Part I

THE DIVINE CONNECTION

"He has made everything beautiful in its time. He has also set eternity in the hearts of men; yet they cannot fathom what God has done from beginning to end."

—Ecclesiastes 3:11

The Cue Ball

He said in a loud voice, "Fear God and give him glory, because the hour of his judgment has come. Worship him who made the heavens, the earth, the sea and the springs of water."

— Revelation 14:7

Several years ago, I hiked through Yosemite National Forest. Yosemite is one of the most beautiful places on earth, 1.3 million acres of the most stunning scenery the planet has to offer, with altitudes ranging from 900 to almost 14,000 feet. Everywhere you look, the view is spectacular. The trees, the wildlife, the mountains and the fresh air force you to pause and appreciate their beauty. The power and glory of God's creation are on full display in Yosemite National Forest.

One day as I was hiking through Yosemite, I noticed a tiny dot on the surface of one of the largest mountain faces, Half Dome. Half Dome is the crown jewel at the eastern end of Yosemite Valley. It rises 4,737 vertical feet from the valley floor to the crest of Half Dome.[1] This tiny dot I saw on the face of Half Dome was barely noticeable and hardly moving, like an ant on a mountain. I continued my hike for another hour, then paused to look back and locate the tiny spot again. When I found it, I saw that it had only moved an inch or so, from my perspective; the dot didn't appear to be making much headway.

This dot was in fact a mountain climber (perhaps even a group of climbers!) scaling the face of Half Dome. Even now it amuses and amazes me to think that people see this massive rock and decide that the best way to spend a sunny day is by toiling up the side of a gigantic mountain trying to defeat nature. Do I even need to ask them why?

Watching the dot's slow progress made me grateful to be standing on solid ground and forced me to pause to admire the insanity of the attempt. That tiny human being scaling the side of Half Dome also helped me appreciate the size and magnificence of the mountain. It helped to put the mountain—and my own life—into perspective.

As I watched, I was brought back to a memory of a college geography lesson. My professor declared that if you were to shrink our planet down to the size of a cue ball, the world would actually be as smooth as a cue ball. Half Dome and all the other mountain peaks, from Nepal's famous Mount Everest, to every rolling hill, would not even be detectable to a human hand running across its surface. The planet is just that enormous.

I then began to think about what the Bible teaches about the size of God and his relationship to the Earth. God's actual size is impossible for man to comprehend, but if we look into the Scriptures, we can begin to formulate an idea.

Who has measured the waters in the hollow of his hand,
   or with the breadth of his hand marked off the heavens?
Who has held the dust of the earth in a basket,
   or weighed the mountains on the scales
   and the hills in a balance?
(Isaiah 40:12)

Only God can measure the waters of the earth in "the hollow of his hand." Just in the little indention in the palm of his hand, God can hold the waters that cover our planet. If he can hold the oceans like a few drops of water, it is no stretch to say that the almighty God can cradle our planet like a cue ball in the palm of his hand. Picture a cue ball in the palm of your hand. What if the cue ball was

Earth and you were God? The image is spectacular, mind-boggling, awe-inspiring.

Now carry that same thought a step further, picturing the cue ball, but also considering that mountain climber toiling up the face of Half Dome. Consider that tiny little speck ascending the face of that huge mountain, on a planet that is shrunk down to the size of a cue ball, resting in the palm of God's hand. The climber is no more significant than a minuscule, microscopic, infinitesimal speck of dust when compared to the glorious size of the almighty God!

This is an illustration using human points of reference, limited by finite thinking and an inadequate vocabulary, that attempts to begin painting a picture of the magnitude and scope of our glorious God. It's a frightening and humbling image. It is safe to say that any time we try to picture God, he is much larger than we could ever grasp or imagine, whether we are just trying to imagine his size, or attempting to understand his sovereignty. God is truly glorious.

A Moment in Time

But do not forget this one thing, dear friends: With the LORD *a day is like a thousand years, and a thousand years are like a day.*
— 2 Peter 3:8

The apostle Peter is trying to help us humans, bound as we are by time, to begin to understand a God who lives in eternity. For God, one day is like a thousand years. For God, the difference between a thousand years and a day is nothing in the span of eternity; however, for us, it is the difference between twenty-four hours and several generations. The apostle Peter is painting a word picture for us. He is trying to help us understand the presence of God in our lifetime as it relates to his eternal life. The difference is magnificent and the image is powerful.

Although the apostle's statement should not be taken too literally, it does help to break it down, word by word, to begin to comprehend the message. If we break this scripture down, that would mean that our lifetime, assuming we reach the average life expectancy of between seventy-two and eighty-four years,[1] is approximately equal to one hour and forty-five minutes in God's day. Chew on that for a second. Our entire lifetime is equal to just one hour and forty-five minutes of God's day. By comparison, mosquitoes live longer than that.[2] To put it another way, our generation will last around 105 minutes in God's day. That is about the time it takes to watch a feature-length movie, and is shorter than the time that passes between two meals.

This is another humbling, yet awe-inspiring thought. How right James was when he said, "You are like a mist that appears for a little while and then vanishes."[3] Our existence is truly nothing more than a flash, a flicker, a blip in eternity. Like water that flows down a river, so our existence flows past God through eternity.

Let me ask you: Have you ever been late for anything, or overslept? Did you ever have an "off" day? A day when you just didn't get anything done, perhaps because you were a bit lazy, or forgot the things you were supposed to do, or just chose to blow off your responsibilities? We've all had days like that. What if God didn't pay attention and had an off day? What if God overslept? A brief lapse on his part could amount to half our lifetime, or worse, our entire lifetime. Generations could go by!

Thankfully, God isn't like man. He doesn't oversleep, he doesn't put things off, he doesn't get distracted. Isaiah 40:28 promises, "He will not grow tired or weary." Praise God that we don't have to worry about him sleeping through our generation.

God doesn't forget about us; he won't leave us out there by ourselves. He knows each one of us. After Noah had been floating around the earth with a boatful of animals for 150 days, the Bible says, "But God remembered Noah."[4] God didn't forget that he had placed Noah on an ark, accompanied by two of every animal on earth. God didn't forget Noah, and he won't forget us. Even though we are microscopic compared to God, he won't forget us.

We are a tiny little speck on a planet the size of a cue ball, sitting in the hand of God, and that tiny little speck's existence only lasts for about an hour and forty-five minutes of one of God's days. Our life is meaningless in the grand scheme of it all. Our insignificance is completely beyond our comprehension—too great for us to fathom. We must stand in awe of the almighty God and praise his glorious name forever and ever!

I have spent the past twenty-five years of my life getting to know the God who can hold the world in the palm of his hand. I have had many ups and downs, with my share of highs and lows, but it seems to me that as each year passes and a new one starts, God is bigger than I could have ever imagined, and I am smaller and less significant than I ever thought. The more time goes by, the more I realize how much I need God's grace and his love, and how little he needs my works and deeds. As I continue in my walk with Christ, I understand that following Jesus is more about who God wants me to *be* and less about what he wants me to *do*. If I am who he wants me to be, then I will naturally do what he wants me to do.

Stay with me for the chapters ahead as we explore what it means to be a microscopic speck on a cue ball in the hand of a mighty God.

A Wise Beginning

As a father has compassion on his children, so the LORD has compassion on those who fear him; for he knows how we are formed, he remembers that we are dust.

— Psalm 103:13–14

We can feel so irrelevant in the universe and so humbled when we bring God into view. With a holy fear and reverent awe, we can wonder: Who am I? Why am I here? What is my purpose? What would God have me to be? My life seems so small and insignificant; I seem inconsequential and unimportant. What can I possibly offer to God that is of any value?

In an attempt to put our significance into perspective, we have to first understand what is truly important to a God who is bigger than our minds could ever fathom. What does he truly care about, and what is he looking for from us?

God worked for six days putting all of the world and its universe together. Everything we can see came from God in one way or another. Proverbs tells us that God began his great works by first creating wisdom, and wisdom speaks to us about God's creation in Proverbs 8:22–31:

"The LORD brought me forth as the first of his works,
*   before his deeds of old;*
I was appointed from eternity,
*   from the beginning, before the world began.*
When there were no oceans, I was given birth,
*   when there were no springs abounding with water;*
before the mountains were settled in place,
*   before the hills, I was given birth,*
before he made the earth or its fields
*   or any of the dust of the world.*
I was there when he set the heavens in place,
*   when he marked out the horizon on the face of the deep,*
when he established the clouds above
*   and fixed securely the fountains of the deep,*
when he gave the sea its boundary
*   so the waters would not overstep his command,*
and when he marked out the foundations of the earth.
*   Then I was the craftsman at his side.*
I was filled with delight day after day,
*   rejoicing always in his presence,*
rejoicing in his whole world
*   and delighting in mankind.*

Wisdom was the first of God's creations; she is always rejoicing in God's presence and delighting in mankind. She was there at his side in the beginning. While God was creating the world, wisdom was "the craftsman at his side" who "rejoiced in his presence." Wisdom rejoiced in the Creator and delighted in the creation.

Proverbs also tells us, "The fear of the LORD is the beginning of wisdom."[1] I can remember a time when my first son was about eleven years old, and I wanted so desperately to connect with him. I had always dreamed of being a great dad and having a close relationship with my children. I wanted to be the main figure in my son's life, and I wanted to be his best friend. I really tried to be on his level, to relate to him and be the "cool" dad. I wanted my son to turn to me before he would turn to someone else. The only problem was that my plan wasn't working. Sometimes my son didn't respect me, nor did he come to me with everything and anything. He treated my words as if they were optional, as if he didn't need to obey.

I remember sharing with a close friend about how my plan wasn't working. I felt like I had known exactly how to raise children until I had some! This particular friend was a great example; he had raised three great Christian children. He told me that my son didn't need a friend. He needed a father. He said that our children don't need someone to try to be cool with them and be their pal, our children need someone to help them through life, guiding them along the way, stepping in to help them make decisions; someone to teach them, train them, and discipline them, preparing them up for adulthood. Lastly (and this is what really hurt), he told me that my son probably didn't want me to be his friend either. He had friends. He wanted and needed a father. It's kind of weird for a father to try to be "cool" with his kids. It only makes the kids disrespectful, and creates a strange dynamic in the relationship. No, children need a father, not a friend.

The difference between a friend and father is that there is a healthy fear present in the relationship with a father. A father is an authority figure—but not just an authority figure—a father loves unconditionally. Our children should *have* a healthy fear of their parents, but they shouldn't *live* in fear of them. Children should never be afraid of their parents, but they should know that disobedience will put them outside the will of their parents and result in some form of teaching, training, or discipline. As the children grow up, they mature in their understanding of the lessons their parents were trying to teach them. They grow in wisdom, and begin to understand that their parents were not trying to make their lives miserable, but that they had their best interests at heart and were training them for life. Then, at this mature stage, the parent and child will now have the ability to become friends.

There are few joys greater in life than when children are grown and they thank their parents for the teaching, training, and discipline they gave them along the way. "A wise son brings joy to his father."[2]

The first step to having a relationship with God is to cultivate a reverent and healthy fear of him within our hearts. Once we have the fear of God, then wisdom can begin to come into our life, because we can see life from the right viewpoint: acknowledging God as our father, knowing that he works all things to help us develop a relationship with him and mature in our walk with him.

To grow in wisdom, we must continue to grasp our insignificance in this universe. We need to take hold of the idea that God doesn't need us for anything. We need to accept the fact that he is complete without us. This is a humbling thought to comprehend, but if we allow ourselves to acknowledge these truths and be moved to the proper respect and reverence for God, then we will be in the right mindset and posture to be of service to him. We will move toward knowledge of God with a submissive and willing spirit. We will finally understand that everything comes down to God's mercy on us, and that the one who created this cue ball that we live on is also a loving father in our lives.

The Humble Creation

By faith we understand that the universe was formed at God's command, so that what is seen was not made out of what was visible.

—Hebrews 11:3

So what is it that God wants from us? What is he guiding us toward? What is he creating in us? We can find a big clue in the book of Genesis and the story of creation. Genesis chapter 1 describes how God created the world. Then Genesis 2:1 says, "Thus the heavens and the earth were completed in all their vast array." That's it! No fanfare, no soaring musical number—just a profound understatement. Creation was completed. Chapter 2 wraps up a few more details, but essentially that's all we get; one chapter of the Bible sums up the creation of the cosmos, our planet, and all life forms on earth. Everything we can see or know was created by God, but all we get from the Bible is one chapter about it (not that we could possibly understand everything involved in creation, even if God tried to spell it out for us!). Think about all that God has left unsaid in the Bible about creation. He left us just one simple chapter that has stood the test of time.

The last time I checked, the Bible is a pretty thick book, and yet God chose to devote just thirty-four verses to creation. God could have filled up the entire Bible depicting the details of creation, and still, we would be getting only a microscopic glimpse of what he did during creation week. He could have filled infinite volumes with descriptions of his great achievement. Instead, God chose to speak about his awesome accomplishment for a few short paragraphs.

What does this tell us about God? Not only is he exceedingly humble—humble beyond human comprehension—but he must not be too concerned about touting his accomplishments. He has given us a simple account about creation that still stands today. So then, to what topics does God assign precious pages of the Bible? Well, let's start by breaking down the books of Genesis and Exodus. God dedicates fifteen chapters to a man who will later be called the father of our faith: Abraham. The life of Abraham's son Isaac gets approximately six chapters, and Isaac's son Jacob gets about ten chapters. God devotes twelve chapters to telling the story of Isaac's son, Joseph. When God raises up Moses to lead the Israelites out of Egypt, he devotes almost all forty chapters of the book of Exodus to Moses' life and leadership.

What can we learn from this? What do all these men have in common? They all had faith in the almighty God. They believed God, and for that reason we are still talking about them today. The precious pages of the Bible are not dedicated to what God can do but what men and women can do with God. Our reverent fear and awe of God should turn into great faith—faith that God can use to accomplish his purposes. In depicting the men and women of the Bible, God does not disguise their humanity. He does not hide the fact that they made mistakes time and again, but he also exposes the faith they put in him. He shows us that these ordinary people had an extraordinary faith.

Do you get the message that God is trying to communicate to us? Yes, he gave his laws and teachings through men like Moses, but he could have just written down his commands and left it at that. The Bible could have been nothing more than a list of rules. Instead, God dedicates valuable pages of the Bible to the lives of great (but imperfect) men and women of faith. We witness Abraham placing his only son on the altar, ready to kill him at God's command; we see Joseph spending fifteen years of his life either in slavery or in prison, holding on to his faith and integrity the entire time. The single greatest thing that shines through their stories is their faith in God.

What is God's point in all this? What is truly important in our lives today? What does God value and look for in us? Does he care most about our careers, our social status, even our personality? No, God is looking for faith, faith like we see in lives of the great men and women of the Bible.

What is important for tiny specks like us humans—miniscule particles of dust that will reside on earth for less than two hours of God's day? Faith in the Almighty! Peter tells us that our faith is "more precious than gold."[1] There is no greater pursuit for us than the pursuit of faith. The world runs after gold and riches, but God tells us that faith is far more valuable. Faith is more precious than anything the world has to offer.

Hebrews 11:16 says that it is not possible to please God if you don't have faith. You can be the nicest person in the world, doing good deeds on the planet, but God won't be impressed with you if you don't have faith. As God stands there, holding the world, populated by all of its microscopic human specks, he wants to see that we believe in him, that we know he exists, and that we seek to know him better every day. Although our eyes don't see him physically, our hearts can see him through faith. This is what is truly precious to our Creator.

Part II

GREATER THAN GOLD

Your faith—of greater worth than gold...
— 1 Peter 1:7

Faith, Not Religion

And without faith it is impossible to please God.
—Hebrews 11:6

One of the accusations levied against the religious world by the non-religious world is that we are always telling people to have faith, but we never teach them *how* to have faith. Faith is a concept that we can all understand in principal, but the application of our faith is where it gets difficult not just to explain, but also to apply; therefore, we end up converting the world to *religion*, but not to *faith*. There are many people in the world who would love to apply some true godly faith in their lives, or even to gain greater faith, if they just knew how. We cannot just tell people to have faith; we need to be teachers of applying faith.

Jesus tells us that if we have faith even as small as a mustard seed, it can grow exceedingly great.[1] The amount of faith is not what's truly important at the beginning of our walk with God. We just need a tiny speck to begin. We just need a crumb so that it can continue to grow. I have heard it said, "We don't need to put great faith in God, we need to start by putting a little faith in a great God." We only need to start with a speck, and God can turn that into greatness.

Again, consider the mountain climber on the Earth the size of a cue ball from Chapter 1. This mountain climber is truly a microscopic dot on the side of the mountain in comparison to the size and magnitude of the almighty God. As God holds the cue-ball-sized world in his hand, we are ridiculously small compared to him. Now consider faith inside that ridiculously small mountain climber, and you can begin to see what God is after. It is faith in our lives that God values; it's faith in our hearts that sets us apart in this vast universe, that distinguishes us from the billions of other tiny specks on this cue ball. It's the faith inside us that can actually become useful to the Father—the faith that is in our hearts and is put in God.

The first thing we must understand is that whatever we do in serving God, we must be very humble. What could insignificant human beings possibly offer to almighty God? He doesn't need anything from us. God does *expect* from us, but he doesn't *need* anything from us. So whatever service we offer to God must be done in absolute humility. We should not expect or assume any favor from him because of what we do, or somehow imagine that God would be in our debt because of the service we offer to him. This principle is just as true when applying our faith. Our faith earns us nothing.

In Luke 17:5–10, when the apostles ask the Lord to increase their faith, Jesus tells them, "If you have faith as small as a mustard seed, you can say to this mulberry tree, 'Be uprooted and planted in the sea,' and it will obey you." However, in the very next verse Jesus tells them a parable about a servant who works in a field all day, and at the end of the day, the master still expects that servant to cook his dinner and wait on him while he eats and drinks. That servant should not expect any special treatment, or think that now he deserves to eat first—he has just done his job. The servant is only doing what the master expects of him, and the servant should not think he will get special treatment for fulfilling his duty.

In the same way, when we apply our faith in God, we should not expect that somehow God will reward us for our act of faith. Rather, we should say, "I am just an unworthy servant. I have only done my duty." We are God's servants, and because of this, we should occupy our time and use our strength to complete the good works God has prepared for us to do. We make the end of one service to God the beginning of another. The servant who has been plowing the field all day, or tending the livestock in the hot sun, still has work to do and duties to fulfill when he gets home at night. We are merely servants employed by God, and we leave it up to him to decide what we should receive from his grace and from his love. God will decide what comforts he chooses to offer, but these comforts come from his grace, and not because we have earned them.

Some Christians refuse to do the work that God requires, or fail to give Christ the praise he deserves, because they feel they have not received the comfort and blessings from God that they deserve. This kind of thinking is wrong. First, we are to apply ourselves in the work God requires and give him the praise, glory, and honor he deserves. Then we will bask in the comforts of his love and feast at his table of blessings.

Jesus himself set us this example, as he came "not...to be served, but to serve."[2] He came among his disciples as a fellow servant, not as the master lording over them. He didn't come to tell everyone what to do and to exercise his authority. He came as a humble servant. During Jesus' days on earth, he didn't lead the disciples with a heavy hand or a clenched fist. He led them by example, and became the servant of all.

In one of the many paradoxes of the Bible, God rewards his faithful children by showing us his favor, and we can live confidently, in joyful anticipation of his kindness. However, we should receive his blessings with gratitude. We should not expect that our faith or works of service somehow put God in our debt, or guarantee us an easy life without hardship. God's blessings are gifts, not wages we have earned. God has no debt to us. We can only expect favor from him because of his own promises. God put himself in debt to his own word—his word that promises his love, his word that promises his blessings to us. His generosity does not change who we are; we are still just unworthy servants doing our duty.

One of the biggest reasons we struggle in our faith—or rather, we struggle in the application of our faith—is that we don't have the correct understanding about the right direction of our faith and how to apply it. In the next chapter we will take a look at how to direct the faith we have.

Directing Our Faith

But as for me and my household, we will serve the LORD.
—Joshua 24:15

The other day I heard a preacher giving a sermon. He told a story about watching a football game with some other Christians. They all liked the same team and got together regularly to watch their team play. During one particular game, their team fell behind in the fourth quarter. It didn't look good. One of the guys expressed doubt about their team being able to pull out the victory. That's when the preacher challenged his friend by saying, "Where's your faith?"

Now, most of us who have been Christians for a while have been challenged in this way at some point. We express doubt, and a fellow Christian asks us, "Where's your faith?" To be honest, "Where's your faith?" is a good question, but it should be applied to the correct situations! The implication in the preacher's story was that we should put our faith in a football team. That we should maintain our faith in the group of men playing on the field. Are we to put our faith in a team? Is that what faithfulness is all about? Are we to put our faith in man? In the preacher's example, if the fan doesn't doubt and continues to keep his faith in his *team,* then the team will somehow pull out the victory. I do not believe this to be the true application of faith. The team will let us down! Maybe not today; maybe today they will pull out the victory and we will cheer and celebrate and somehow feel better about ourselves, but eventually they will let us down. Man always does. Man is fallible, and will often let us down. We are never to put our faith in man.

Here's something else I don't put my faith in: my leaders. (It's okay. Take a deep breath and stay with me, I'm not about to teach rebellion here.) Do I love and respect my leaders? Of course! Do I want to make their work a joy, and am I willing to imitate the faith that they display? Absolutely! But I don't put my faith in them. I put my faith in God. God is the one in control, and God alone. He's the one who knows what's best. He knows the motives and intentions of humans. He is sovereign over everything, and he is perfect. Man is not. To put our faith in anything other than God is fruitless, pointless, and could even be considered idolatrous. Many may disagree with me, saying, "But we should have faith in our leaders," but my Bible teaches that faith in anything other than God will fail. Faith in man will not lead to anything but disappointment. Those who choose to put their faith in man are destined for a spiritual rollercoaster, riding the ups and downs of a sinful humanity.

Certainly, some leaders are better than others, and some set a better example than others. They should be respected, imitated and obeyed as they lead us in Christ,[1] but even so, our faith remains in God, not in man. There is an important distinction between the righteous attitude of submitting to God by following the authorities he has established, striving to make their work a joy,[2] versus the ungodly act of putting your faith in the leader himself. Putting too much faith in people has caused many Christians to fall away from God and lose their faith entirely. People have chosen to put their faith in their leaders, and if their leaders fail them, they lose their faith in God. Had these people chosen to put their faith in God only, then they would not have fallen so hard when their leaders proved to be what they are—human.

We are to trust in God, and know that God has put leaders in our lives. We can also be confident that God will deal with any leaders who don't honor him with their service. I'll use an example that was just as touchy for Christians in the first-century church as it is for us today: the giving of contribution. It doesn't get much more personal than when we talk about our money! People who put too much faith in people may say, "I trust the leader and don't worry about what happens to the contribution." Or on the opposite extreme, someone may say, "I don't trust my leader, so I am not going to give my contribution." Both attitudes are wrong and totally man-focused. If we put our faith in God, then we don't have to worry because we know that God will deal with anyone who misuses God's money. He may not deal with them right away, but we know that he will deal with them just as he will deal with all of us: "at the proper time." I personally would not want to misuse God's money! God sees everything and will bring it all to light. If we put our faith in God, we don't have to worry.

I remember a time shortly after I became a Christian. I was attending a small group Bible discussion every week on the campus of the University of Colorado. I was completely engaged with the group. The leader of the Bible discussion, Bruce, had become one of my heroes and closest friends. He stood out to me as a shining example of a Christian life that I wanted to imitate, but I knew I had a long way to go to become like him. He seemed to have wise answers for everything and a remarkable peace about him. I was eager to attend our Bible discussion, as everything was new and fresh for me. Each week presented me with new challenges for growth in my faith.

One night, Bruce walked into our meeting, sat down in front of everyone and said, "I don't believe in the God that I have been serving anymore." He got up and walked out, and we never saw him again. We were shocked and speechless. Bruce's decision not only disturbed everyone in my discussion group, but it also rocked our entire campus ministry. Several other Christians in our group ended up leaving God as a result of Bruce's declaration. Bruce's sudden desertion challenged me to my core. What did I believe? What tied me to the life that I was now living? Was I here because of the people or because of my relationship with God? Could I hang on to my faith in God no matter what came my way? I spent the next several weeks wrestling with my foundational beliefs and resolving that I would be committed to God and God alone.

The Bible teaches us that "love always trusts."[3] I know that I was meant to trust Bruce as my leader and to love him as my brother in Christ, but I could only do this because I had first put my faith in God. I learned the hard way that it is one thing to trust people; it is another thing for our faith to *depend* upon them. I would say that it is my faith in God that *allows* me now to trust my leaders. We can trust others when we first put our faith in God. Our faith in God allows us to trust others, but even so, we are never called to put our faith in man. Or to put it another way, our faith in God does not depend upon man's actions. The church is no place to doubt and contradict leaders. The church is no place to condemn and judge others, especially those over us, but know this one thing: God is in control! He knows all, sees all, and judges everyone according to his perfect righteousness. We can have peace because we first put our faith in God.

So the next time you are watching your favorite team play, or you are listening to an amazing lesson from a leader you admire and respect, you can be at peace in your heart because you have your faith securely in God, no matter what the future may bring.

Faith Applied

"When the Son of Man comes, will he find faith on the earth?"
– Luke 18:8

When Jesus comes back, we do not want to be found without faith. We do not want to be found having not trusted in God, and not fully believing that he exists. When he returns and brings the end of time, we want to be counted among those who have faith. Even though we have not seen him, we believe in him and are living a life of faith because of him. Living with faith is the challenge that eludes so many people.

The religious are always telling others to have faith, but are often guilty of not teaching them *how* to have this faith. We have all heard that faith is the key and the answer. We have all heard it said, "You just need faith." We know that faith will save us from this world and all of its struggles.

Many people come to great change in their life because they have studied the Bible and learned about God. They study the Scriptures, and as a result they change their lives. They join a new fellowship, begin to attend church regularly, and generally become better people as a result of their developing faith, but even so, do they have the faith of the Bible? Will their faith be truly relevant in this life and carry on to the next? Will they cultivate the kind of faith that separates them from a lost world? Can they—and we—really claim to live by faith?

We first have to define faith. We need a definition that we can understand and apply, a definition that has stood the test of time and held up through generations. We can look in the Bible to find examples of faith. We can see great men and women throughout generations who have applied faith in God, and we can witness through the Scriptures the outcome of their faith, but their lives are only examples of this faith. In order to understand faith, we have to look at the definition given to us by God. One of the clearest definitions the Bible gives is found in Hebrews 11:1: "Now faith is being sure of what we hope for and certain of what we do not see."

What a glorious statement! It gives us a small window into a true definition of faith. This one sentence opens for us a great understanding—one that has eluded so many. Here we have faith explained to us and defined for us.

For a great part of my Christianity, I have tried to apply my faith by focusing on two key elements of this verse: that faith is what we *hope for* and is something we *do not see*. It is not entirely incorrect to focus on these two aspects of this verse. We all have things that we hope for—things that we cannot yet see. We assign them a place in our hearts as things that we desperately desire, and we picture them in our minds because they cannot be seen; however, this limited understanding of faith can leave us falling short in our relationship with God. I have found that when I approach faith as something I hope for, then I find myself in a place that is almost the equivalent of *wishing* for something. I wish for things to happen in my life, I desire to see them fulfilled, but this kind of hope really has nothing to do with faith. This kind of wishful dreaming is akin to the hope people have when they buy a lottery ticket. They buy the ticket in the hope of winning. They don't necessarily believe they will win the lottery, but they hope they will—or rather, they wish they will win.

For many years I lived with this type of faith in my life, which is really is no faith at all. I hoped I would get a better job, I hoped my relationship with my neighbors would change, I hoped I would have courage and strength, I hoped my children would become Christians.

I can remember a time in my life when I was desperately looking for a job. I had a newborn son, and bills were mounting. I would have taken anything—any job that would help pay bills and put food on the table. At the time, my faith was more like anxiety. I was wishful, not faithful.

We hope for better jobs, better relationships, character changes—for things in our lives to be different—but are we really being faithful about those things, or are we just nurturing a common, everyday wish? Do we really have an active faith in a real God, or are our prayers just like the wishful thinking of the godless?

To have true faith, we must take a deeper look into Hebrews 11:1 to begin to understand the keys to unlocking true faith—the kind of faith that pleases God and catches his attention.

Finishing the Faith Verse

*Now faith is being sure of what we hope for and certain of what
we do not see.*

—Hebrews 11:1

I have come to realize that I have spent many years focusing on the
wrong parts of Hebrews 11:1. Having faith does not mean that we
only hope for something that we do not see. Faith is something we
hope for, but it is so much more than that. The key to understanding
this verse and the concept of biblical faith lies in two key words:
"sure" and "certain."

Faith is more than just hoping—we are to be *sure* and *certain* of
what we hope for! How did I miss those two words for such a long
time? This is where I was off in my understanding of faith, and where
I was truly lacking in my spiritual life. I was not "sure" and "certain"
in my relationship with God and in the requests I put before him.
I had been "wishy-washy" in my spiritual walk, and so I had a
tendency to waver through unbelief after I prayed for something.
I only "wished" for things in my life, but I never really had faith.
I would pray for things and hope to receive them, but then many
times would waver in my belief.

What do you do when you are sure of something? You act. To use a simple example, if someone throws a ball at your head and you are certain it is going to hit you, what do you do? You either put your hands up to catch the ball, or you duck out of the way. Standing still, waiting to be clobbered, is not an option! Doing nothing is not an option. When we are certain of a situation's outcome, then we will always proceed accordingly. Webster's dictionary defines "sure" as "having or showing no doubt or hesitancy."[1] Being sure is having a confident certainty. We do not waver when we are sure. We do not drift through a maze of uncertainty. We don't vacillate. To be sure is to act and not doubt. The definition of "certain" is "determined, reliable, not to be doubted, unquestionable."[2] Being certain is positively knowing that something is true. The knowledge that something is true should allow us to act without first seeing evidence. We already know the outcome, so we go ahead and act. Faith is to know something to be true before it happens. We are "certain of what we do not see."

If we are sure or we have confident certainty that God will grant our request, then we have no choice but to act on our certainty. If we are sure, then we will move in the direction of our confidence. We will live as if it has happened or will undoubtedly happen. When Jesus performed a miracle, who was amazed? It wasn't Jesus, it was the people around him! Jesus already knew the miracle would take place. He didn't look over his shoulder to see if it actually happened, and then pump his fist in the air in surprise and relief. Jesus didn't give high fives to the other apostles after a healing as if to say, "I can't believe I just did that!" or "Phew, I'm glad that worked!" He knew it would happen, and so he was never shocked. He gave the glory to God for accomplishing amazing miracles, but even so, he was not surprised by God's accomplishments. True faith in God is never surprised, but always amazed. Jesus tells us:

> *"I tell you the truth, if anyone says to this mountain, 'Go, throw yourself into the sea,' and does not doubt in his heart but believes that what he says will happen, it will be done for him. Therefore I tell you, whatever you ask for in prayer, believe that you have received it, and it will be yours." (Mark 11:23-24)*

If we tell a mountain to go throw itself into the sea, and don't doubt the outcome, then we will run to get out of the way of the tidal wave. We will act on the belief that the mountain will be uprooted and tossed into the sea.

The key to this verse is that Jesus tells us to "believe that we have received it"—we *have received* it—past tense. Then we are to know that it will be ours. It will be done. It has already been done. Period, end of sentence. We should not act *as if* it will happen, but *knowing* that it will happen! If I am sure that the ball is going to hit me in the head, then I will act accordingly, no hesitation. I have to act based on this fact coming to pass. I cannot wait to see what happens. I must act. Faith works the same way: We must act, and so we act in faith!

Today, we have turned faith into a position of weakness. Once we have tried everything else, as a last resort we say, "Well, I have faith," as if this is the proper religious response to a difficult situation. We may claim that we have faith, but too often our "faith" springs from some religious duty. We claim we have faith because it is the good Christian response, but not because we are "absolutely certain."

Do you ever stop to think that your life unfolds the way it does because that's exactly how you believed it would happen? If you believe that things will never work out for you, then has it occurred to you that you are only getting what you believe? If you believe that your boss will never like you, your husband will never change, or you will never get married, then you may be getting exactly what you believe!

We can also get hung up on the kinds of things we ask God for. We don't want to ask God for something because we believe our request is "unspiritual," but can you tell me what is spiritual about asking a mountain to throw itself into the sea? I can't find one thing spiritual about telling a mountain to go throw itself into the sea, but that is exactly the example Jesus uses to make his point.

I believe Jesus is opening a door to a world of faith that we have a hard time going through. We tell ourselves that God doesn't really care about the mundane, "unspiritual" things in our lives. We like to think that he only cares about what's really important—but again

I ask you, of what spiritual importance is it for a mountain to be thrown into the sea? The only thing I can find meaningful in asking a mountain to throw itself into the sea is that we, God's children, would ask for it, and that God, our Father, would grant it out of love for us. The important thing about the request is that we, God's children, would ask and believe.

Our faith is made powerful when we are *sure* and *certain*. When we act upon our prayers, God's power unfolds before us. Faith is putting our trust in God beyond what we can see, beyond what our senses would tells us. Faith is not preceded by sight. Faith doesn't wait to see everything clearly. Faith moves first, then sees the power of God unfold before our waiting eyes.

If You, Then God

In the morning, O LORD, you hear my voice; in the morning I lay my request before you and wait in expectation.

—Psalm 5:3

About halfway through the writing of this book, I noticed a strange phenomenon in my life: My clothes were all getting too small. I thought that something must be happening in the wash. My clothes must be shrinking because they were being washed differently, or some new detergent must be affecting my wardrobe—that must be the problem. But then something alarming happened. I took my family on a vacation to Hawaii. We'd had this trip planned for a long while, and I was looking forward to a nice week of rest and relaxation on a beach in Waikiki. My wife had decided that since we would be on a beautiful island, we should get new family pictures taken. We'd be in the sun with beautiful scenery, looking tan, rested and refreshed. (My oldest son and I have now mastered the art of taking family pictures: If we wear what we're told, sit where we're told, and smile on cue, then the ordeal is shorter and less painful. It's taken many years, but we are now sufficiently brainwashed to survive family-portrait sessions with minimal trauma.)

When we returned from our vacation, my wife selected the pictures she liked, blew them up and placed the different portraits around the house. When I came home from work and saw the photos around the house, my first thought was, "Beautiful family, but who's the fatso standing next to my wife?" Some chubby guy had taken my place.

Needless to say, my clothes weren't mysteriously shrinking in the wash, and no one was playing a trick on me. I had put on some serious weight. At five feet ten inches tall, I was circling around 205 pounds. I had never weighed more than two hundred pounds before, but now that number was my consistent companion. My waist had grown to the point where the buttons on my size thirty-eight pants were screaming for mercy. If you were to ask someone to guess what my occupation was, I believe their first thought would be Bacon Smuggler. I needed to lose some weight.

The trouble was, I didn't feel like doing anything except eating. I didn't want to run, lift weights or eat healthy food. I had no ambition or energy to get started. The only thing that motivated me to put down the Cheetos was the haunting image of some stranger standing next to my wife in our family photos.

With visions of the family portrait dancing before my eyes, I set out for my first run in a long time. It was a gorgeous day: a perfect seventy-two degrees, a slight breeze and, to my dismay, no chance of rain. That's the trouble with living in California—the weather will never give you an excuse to miss a workout.

I headed out, putting one foot in front of another, stewing the whole time over how much I hated running. I didn't have the bounce or the drive that I had when I was younger, and now the experience was miserable. My knees cracked, my joints ached, my lungs wheezed. But still I plodded along, until the toe of my shoe caught on a crack in the sidewalk. Time slowed, just like in a cartoon. I was going down. I could see the pavement coming up to meet my face, and there was nothing I could do to stop it. Now, if this had happened in my younger days, a simple stumble like this wouldn't have been a big deal—my cat-like reflexes would have taken over and my feet would have sprung back under my body in a split second to avert disaster and get me back on my way. But this wasn't one of my younger days.

I went down like an elephant in shackles. First my knee, then my hip, followed by an elbow and a shoulder—before I knew which end was up, I flew into a full somersault, finally coming to a landing on my side. There I was, lying on the ground, all alone; no one came out of their homes to see what the commotion was—after all why would they? People are used to the occasional earthquake in Southern California—that day, I just happened to be the epicenter.

Without even thinking, I got up and began a slow jog for home. My knee was a little bloody and my hip a little sore, but that was it— no internal bleeding, no concussion or broken bones—just a little raspberry on my knee and a sore hip. My injuries were minimal, but I had automatically hit the GPS for home. I stopped and thought, "What am I doing?" Why was it so easy to just give up? Why was it so automatic to turn around? As I shuffled home, I had an epiphany: I no longer wanted anything to be difficult. I no longer wanted anything to be difficult or challenging. I had pre-programmed my brain to take the path marked "easy," and so I was only doing what I had prepared myself to do: to take the first excuse that came along, and quit.

I stopped on my way home and turned back around. I set out again for the run I had intended, but with a clarity I hadn't had for a long time. I realized that if I was going to get in shape, then it was going to mean that I had to take the first difficult step. It would require me to set out in the direction I wanted, and I would eventually arrive where I wanted to be—but no one would do it for me, and it wouldn't be easy.

After several months of diet and exercise, I have lost twenty pounds, and exercising is something I look forward to. It's no longer something I dread, as my body has taken over where my motivation had been lacking. I still have a little ways to go, but I am confident that by setting my course in the right direction, I have committed to a lifestyle that I will keep up for the rest of my life.

For so many people, their mindset about their walk with God mirrors the way I had been thinking about exercise. Their relationship with God is an if-then statement: "If God, then I..." We think, "*If* God would" (fill in the blank), "*then* I would" (fill in the blank). "*If* God would do what I want, *then* I would really believe in him."

We want God to act first, and then we tell ourselves that we will move forward in faith. We don't want to take the first painful step in our relationship with God, we want him to do it first. The truth is, God already has initiated by sending his Son, and now it's our turn to act! We have to step out in faith if we want a personal relationship with him, if we want to see him work in our lives.

Have you ever said something as simple as this: "*If* God would move the curtain that I'm staring at right now, *then* I would be convinced that he exists"? It may sound silly, but many of us have prayed superstitious prayers like this! We all want to see God move first, then we will believe—or at least we think we would believe. And then, once God proves himself to us, we think we would act upon our faith: *If* God would give me that job, girlfriend, boyfriend, pay raise, car, husband, wife, *then* I would be more faithful, more loving, more giving, more committed, and more spiritual.

The Bible teaches that faith doesn't work that way! God's way is, *If* you, *then* God. Jesus tells us,

> *"If anyone chooses to do God's will, [then] he will find out whether my teaching comes from God or whether I speak on my own."* (John 7:17, addition mine)

We are called to act first in our faith, then the glory of God will be revealed in our lives. We have to take the first step, just like the Israelites who were called to cross the Jordan River. The river didn't stop flowing until the priests carrying the ark set foot in the Jordan.

> *Now the Jordan is at flood stage all during harvest. Yet as soon as the priests who carried the ark reached the Jordan and their feet touched the water's edge, the water from upstream stopped flowing. It piled up in a heap a great distance away...* (Joshua 3:15–16)

They were called to act first. Imagine the bizarre scene as the entire nation of Israel lined up behind the priests and walked toward the flood-swollen banks of the Jordan River. To an outsider, they must have looked like a nation of crazy people on a suicide mission! God didn't move until the priests' feet were wet, until the ark of the covenant crossed the water's edge. The Israelites had to act on their faith, and then they saw the glory of God part the waters—then they walked across the Jordan River.

God is looking for those who will act on their faith, not just sit back and say, "I have faith." Faith is acting on what we expect, without seeing any physical evidence. We act first, knowing it is already done.

What good is it, my brothers, if a man claims to have faith but has no deeds? Can such faith save him?...In the same way, faith by itself, if it is not accompanied by action, is dead.

But someone will say, "You have faith; I have deeds."

Show me your faith without deeds, and I will show you my faith by what I do. You believe that there is one God. Good! Even the demons believe that—and shudder...You see that a person is justified by what he does and not by faith alone." (James 2:14, 17-19, 24)

Faith is not just a feeling, it is an action. If we have faith and act on our faith, then we can step into the water and watch God's miracles unfold.

Men of Certainty

This is what the ancients were commended for.
– Hebrews 11:2

Hebrews 11 has often been called the "Faith Hall of Fame." After defining faith as "being sure of what we hope for and certain of what we do not see," the chapter goes on to recount the exploits of men and women of great faith. Let's look at some of the men and women of faith in Hebrews 11—people who acted according what they believed, who were confident, fully certain of God in their lives. God commends them as righteous people who championed our faith. Their faith is what we are called to imitate today.

As we have seen, when we read the word *faith*, we don't always have the right understanding of the concept—*God's* understanding. I have taken the liberty of rewriting some verses, employing the definition of faith given to us by the author of Hebrews. I hope this exercise will help to change our definition of faith so that we no longer interpret it as mere positive thinking or optimism; instead, we will understand faith as being completely confident, absolutely certain, and fully assured that what we hope and pray for will happen.

Take a fresh look at Hebrews 11:

Hebrews 11:4: Abel, because *he was absolutely convinced there was a God,* offered God a better sacrifice than Cain did.

Hebrews 11:5: Enoch, because *he walked in total assurance with God,* was taken from the earth.

Hebrews 11:7: Noah, because *he was completely sure about what God told him,* in holy fear built the ark to save his family.

Hebrews 11:8–9: Abraham, when called to go to a place he would later receive as his inheritance, *was absolutely, positively certain that God would take care of him,* and so he obeyed and went, even though he did not know where he was going. He made his home in a foreign country *because had no doubt in God at all*; he lived in tents, as did Isaac and Jacob, who were heirs with him of the same promise.

Hebrews 11:11–12: And Abraham, who was *100% confident in God,* even though he was past age—and Sarah herself was barren—was enabled to become a father because *he was fully and completely certain* of what God had promised him. And so, from this one man, and he as good as dead, came descendants as numerous as the stars in the sky and as countless as the sand on the seashore.

Hebrews 11:13: All these people were still living *with absolute confidence in God* when they died.

Hebrews 11:14–16: People who say such things *live with complete certainty in God,* and show that they are *confidently* looking for a country of their own. If they had been thinking of the country they had left, they would have had opportunity to return. Instead, they were longing for a better country—a heavenly one. Therefore God is not ashamed to be called their God, for he has prepared a city for them.

It makes a difference, reading these familiar scriptures worded a little differently, doesn't it? When we consider our biblical heroes in light of the Hebrews 11:1 definition of faith, we realize just how faithful these people were! Let's take a closer look at the faith of one of the most famous men in the Old Testament, the man after God's own heart: David.

David Was a Sure Man

David, the shepherd boy who became king, provides us with a riveting example of faith. When David stepped onto the battlefield against the Philistine giant Goliath, David was a scrawny kid, probably just sixteen or seventeen years old. He had been tending sheep, so he wasn't in fighting shape; he was not a trained soldier, so he would hardly be perceived as a threat to anyone—certainly not to a military hero like Goliath. Armor wouldn't fit him, and a sword was too much for him to handle. He wasn't respected by his brothers, let alone the other soldiers. He was qualified to look after sheep, not fight giants.

One morning, Goliath came out, as he did every day, and shouted his defiance against the armies of Israel and against their God. His blasphemies had become quite routine to the soldiers of Israel, but on this one particular day something different happened, something that would change the course of history and set Israel in a new direction. The Scriptures, in typical understatement, say that on this particular day, Goliath shouted his usual insult, "and David heard it."[1] *David heard*, and everything changed. David—a man who was completely certain that there was a God in heaven, a God who heard what Goliath was shouting every day to the armies of Israel, a God who could break Goliath like a twig—heard, and decided to act.

When David walked onto the battlefield to face Goliath, the nine-foot-tall giant, the battle-tested warrior, he wasn't afraid, because he was absolutely, positively, certain that God would grant him victory over "this uncircumcised Philistine."[2] If he wasn't completely confident in God, do you think David would have stepped out onto that battlefield? Not unless he had a death wish! Without God in the picture, David would have been just another crazy person, but he was fully certain in God! It doesn't take an army to change the course of history; it takes one person who is absolutely, positively certain in God.

We can see David's faith in his prayers. David prayed with absolute certainty. Think about the things that we pray about, the things that we ask for, and how we pray. We basically pray by asking for the things that we want to be different in our lives. We offer up the usual prayers of, "God, please help me to (fill in the blank)," or "God, please change (fill in the blank)." Perhaps we will spend some time praising God and thanking him for all he has done before we ask him for what we want. We confess our sins and ask God's forgiveness. All these elements of prayer are good, and we should continue to do them, but there is a difference in the way a faithful person like David prays.

Consider this prayer of David's:

It is God who arms me with strength
    and makes my way perfect.
He makes my feet like the feet of a deer;
    he enables me to stand on the heights.
He trains my hands for battle;
    my arms can bend a bow of bronze.
You give me your shield of victory,
    and your right hand sustains me;
    you stoop down to make me great.
You broaden the path beneath me,
    so that my ankles do not turn.
I pursued my enemies and overtook them;
    I did not turn back till they were destroyed.
(Psalm 18:32-37)

Now let's be honest. If you or I offered up a prayer like this, how would we word it? We would probably say something like:

"God, please help me in battle. Help me to be strong, and show me the right way. Make me fast, and help me to defeat the enemy. Help me in the battle. Please give me victory."

We are offering up similar requests, but in a way that doesn't claim the victory in the prayer. We pray with doubt. If you look at David's prayer, it's a prayer of faith. He prays as though the things he is expressing have already happened. In confidence he says, "my arms can bend a bow of bronze," and "you give me your shield of victory." David prays as if God has already done these things—in fact, in the eyes of David's faith, God has already done these things for him, and David is confident that God will continue to give him the victory. Faith doesn't spend time wondering. Faith doesn't spend time waiting. Faith accepts and acts. Faith in God is instant and immediate. "God, you make me strong." Period! There really is no waiting when it comes to faith. God gives to his children who believe.

Say, for example, that you want more joy in your life. You can pray, "God, please make me joyful," or you can pray with faith: "God you make me joyful. You give me great joy in my life. I celebrate and praise you because of the wonderful joy you give me. When I am down, you lift me up. When I am being beaten up by the world, you grant me great joy through your Spirit, and I praise you, God. I thank you that you hear my prayer!" This is a prayer that doesn't wonder, doesn't speculate, and doesn't wait. This is a prayer that offers immediate thanks to God, believing he has already given the answer.

Cue Ball Victory

The Bible says that God has made his children "to be a kingdom and priests to serve our God, and they will reign on the earth."[1]

For so many of us, this is a foreign concept. Do you feel like you reign on the earth? Do you live with the power of God every day? Do you go from one victory to the next? My guess is that most of us don't live like that. We settle for struggling through each day. We struggle to get out of bed and just make it; we settle for surviving each day.

I can remember a time, right after my first son was born, when my wife and I were living on Staten Island, New York, and we were struggling to get through each day. We had no money and the future seemed very bleak. I would tell you that we lived on beans and rice, but we couldn't afford the beans to go in the rice. For a short time we used a towel to wrap around our son instead of diapers because diapers cost too much. I was looking for work, but in the meantime, I worked telemarketing and valet parking. My wife commuted every day into New Jersey, working a full-time job, and after she paid for gas, tolls, and childcare, she brought home about $40–$60 a week. It wasn't much, but we needed it desperately. At last I decided to fill out the paperwork to apply for government support. I could not believe that my life had gotten to this point, but I couldn't see any other way out. I could sympathize with Job when he said, "My days have passed, my plans are shattered, and so are the desires of my heart."[2] I didn't know if I had the strength to get myself out of the situation I had put my family in. I had read that we are "meant to reign on the earth," but to me it was only words.

It was then, in my desperate pleas to God, that I realized we do not reign on earth with money, prestige, or power, but we reign on earth through faith, through the fact that we have a direct connection to the creator of it all. As Deuteronomy 4:7 says, "What other nation is so great as to have their gods near to them the way the LORD our God is near to us whenever we pray to him?" We reign because our God, the creator of heaven and earth, is right there with us. He listens to our prayers and knows our every need. He teaches us and wants us to grow as his children, and our biggest area for growth is our faith. We go through the hard times because he cares for us, and we all have a lot to change if we are to become like his son. Although he could allow us to win the lottery or find other easy ways out of our trials, the easy way is not always the best thing for us.

Abraham, Isaac, Jacob, Joseph, and David all reigned on earth. God is the glorious, magnificent, and powerful God. He created the universe. He can do anything he wants, and he gives to those who ask—those who ask and do not doubt.

Think about the things that we ask for. Think about the way that we pray. We basically pray the same way every day (and we're doing more than the average "Christian" if we pray every day). Think about the things that you want to see changed in your life and the things that you want to see happen. We offer up prayers to God, and we hope that we see a change. We want to be good Christians, so we say the right things, but do we really have faith that God will act, or are we just being optimistic, practicing positive thinking? Are we praying with the certainty that knows that God will answer even before we finish our prayer?

Consider another example. Let's say you would like for God to bless you with courage in your life. You may say a prayer like, "God, please give me courage. Help me to be courageous in every situation." (It's hard to expound upon a vague prayer like this.)

Now consider a prayer for courage that comes from faith—a prayer like David's. It would sound something like this:

"God, you give me courage, for I am afraid at times to do the things you want me to do. I am afraid to live the life that I need to live, but I trust in you and I am not afraid of anything, because you give me the confidence and the strength I need in every situation. You make me strong and courageous. I am a child of yours, and you love me and do these things in my life. You lead me, guide me, and show me the way. I trust in you and will not fear. Even though I feel incomplete and imperfect at times, you guide me through. I find victory in your son Jesus, and I praise you all the days of my life!"

To be honest, just writing a faithful prayer like that makes me want to continue the prayer further. I feel it brings me closer to God to continue to claim the life that God has given me. It makes me want to declare the glories of God and live my life with great faith. I don't want to sit back wishing things would get better in my life.

I look back now on my earlier years and remember the struggles we had as a family, and today I am grateful to God, not just because he brought us to a better place financially, but I'm grateful that he allowed us to go through those times to show us that true riches come from faith in the almighty God! We are rich because the creator of the universe is right there for us.

Now I live my life and want to see amazing things happen because I am *sure* and *certain* in our almighty God. I accept what his word says. I will pray with true faith, faith that inspires me to act.

My prayer is that your heart will also know and understand this faith so you can live a life that brings glory to God and allows you to reign on earth!

Faith, Not Time

"Until man duplicates a blade of grass, nature can laugh at his so-called scientific knowledge."

—*Thomas Edison*

It wasn't long after we hit our lowest point that I began to work in manufacturing. Many of our hardest days seem like they were just yesterday, but time has passed quickly, and I have now worked in the manufacturing business for fifteen years. I manage and oversee a number of operations, including Product Development, Quality Control, and Production Planning. My primary focus is on toys, and although I manufacture other products as well, most of our products are toy-related and are made in factories throughout Asia.

One of the most important aspects of manufacturing toys is safety testing. We send our products out to a certified testing lab, where technicians perform any number of safety and quality tests. Some of these tests require that we determine the effects of time on a product. How will sunlight, moisture, chlorine, vibration, and motion affect the product over time? Unfortunately, we do not have the luxury of waiting a year or two to find out, so we have to recreate the effects of time in a condensed period of time. So we perform aging tests on our products. We expose them to degradation factors.

We may apply salt, heat, or a chemical that simulates the long-term effects of time, but in a much shorter period.

We tend to think of time as absolute—that it is a predetermined factor in our lives and therefore we must accept it as such. Time will be what it is, and we are subject to it. However, just like in an aging test, the elements of time can be manipulated and distorted. And yet we often allow time to affect our faith because we see time as absolute.

If you were to draw a timeline indicating how most people's faith grows or shrinks in relation to the passage of time, "time" and "faith" would be on opposite ends of that line. We are usually more faithful when we have more time, but as time seems to run out, so does our faith. We are not worried at the beginning of the month, because we have faith in God. We believe that God will help us pay all our bills, or give us that new job we so desperately seek—we have "faith" that something will work out. We're happy and faithful, but as time goes on, we find ourselves starting to slip in our confidence. With every tick of the clock, we become less confident, less faithful, and more fearful.

Recently I watched a TV program that estimated the origin of a species to be around sixty million years ago. They were saying that this particular species came to existence "around" sixty million years ago. I mean, come on. Really? You expect me to believe that we can estimate the origin of something going back sixty million years? *Sixty million* years? Actually, they said between forty million and sixty million; they threw in a buffer of twenty million years just to be safe. I appreciate that they added this, because I don't think forty million years would have been enough to completely impress me with the accuracy of their calculations. Science uses its tools to measure time, but just as product testers can simulate the affect of time on a product by manipulating the environment, don't you think the God of the heavens and earth, the designer of all things, could have worked this into creation?

Science, in general, likes to add time to the end of things it cannot explain. If forty million years won't work for you, then add another twenty million to it. Who could possibly question that?

Who can verify something that happened forty to sixty million years ago? I am not trying to put down science. I am all in favor of science, but I only favor science in its *discovery* of the mysteries that God has put in place, not in its *definition* of the world.

Let's say, for example, that you have three scientists walking through a field, and they come upon a table with a set of four chairs. Now, these three scientists have never seen a table with a set of four chairs before (work with me). They will spend some time analyzing their findings and applying their hypotheses and scientific thinking. Now, these three scientists may discover many ways that mankind can use a table and a set of four chairs, and for this we applaud science, as we should. Science has discovered something that will help mankind tremendously; we no longer have to eat on the floor because science has discovered that this table and set of four chairs can be extremely useful. But science cannot take credit for creating the table and chairs—that belongs to the designer of the table and chairs.

All kidding aside, think of the many discoveries we benefit from every day because of science. The next time you go to the doctor's office and they don't use leeches to cure your ills, you can thank science for progress!

But I believe that scientists err when they take their analyses a step too far. It is one thing to study the uses and construction of a table and chairs; it is another thing to say, "It must have taken sixty million years for this table and set of four chairs to be formed. First, there had to be a torrential rain about fifty million years ago that flooded the whole land, and then a drought about ten million years ago, followed by a deep freeze, and then finally, we arrived at this table and set of four chairs." The problem with this theory is that the builder of the table and set of four chairs is standing off to the side, out of sight, saying, "No, dummies. I created it. It took about a day." Isn't the creation of it obvious? Doesn't the order of things cry out that there is a creator of all things?

I once heard an analogy that compared the concept of life starting by random chance, without a designer, to taking a wristwatch apart, breaking it down into all of its pieces, throwing all the pieces into a bag, shaking it up, and then expecting the watch to come together and keep perfect time. Not a chance! It takes a watchmaker putting the pieces together, then setting and winding the watch, to make it work. How much more the world, and living, breathing beings! It takes a creator putting all the pieces together to make it all work.

So time is on one end of the line, and faith is on the other. This helps us to understand what God meant in Exodus 3. He had commanded Moses to go and speak to Pharaoh, but Moses asked,

> *"Suppose I go to the Israelites and say to them, 'The God of your fathers has sent me to you,' and they ask me, 'What is his name?' Then what shall I tell them?"*
>
> *God said to Moses, "I AM WHO I AM. This is what you are to say to the Israelites: 'I AM has sent me to you.'"*[1]

I'll put that in modern English for you: God *just is*. Deal with it!

All of the world's feeble arguments against God are pointless. He's the creator hiding just out of plain sight. He just is. He is "the Alpha and the Omega, the Beginning and the End,"[2] meaning that he is not bound in time like we are. God is outside of time. He created it. We are merely subject to his rules. Time began for us when Adam sinned in the garden. Death entered the world, and so the clock started ticking. Death put us on this treadmill of time, and only faith can get us off. God just is. He is the great I AM! I had read that passage in Exodus many times, but then one day the profundity of it hit me like a ton of bricks. The greatness of this one simple statement, just two words—*I am*. God is, and "we cannot do anything against the truth, but only for the truth."[3] We just have to deal with it!

The challenge for every Christian is to step outside of time, get away from the things we see, leave a life controlled by circumstance, and step into a life that lives with faith—with absolute certainty in God! As he is creator of life and time, who knows the past and future, God can supersede the constraints of time to accomplish his will. And so we can have confidence that even when time seems set against us, our faith is in the one who is greater than time, and he is on our side.

And now let's take a look at a man whose life is an example of absolute certainty in God.

A Sure Man

Elijah was a man just like us.
— James 5:17

Nothing is known of him before he appears in 1 Kings 17:1. His introduction to us is quite abrupt. We don't know how he was called to be a prophet, nor when. The only thing we know about Elijah is that he shows up on the scene during the reign of one of the more ruthless and callous kings of Israel, King Ahab.

Ahab was the seventh king of Israel. Known for his evil behavior, he added to the sins of his fathers: "Ahab son of Omri did more evil in the eyes of the LORD than any of those before him."[1] He was married to Jezebel, a heathen princess, daughter of the king of the Sidonians. Jezebel was so evil that her name today is still synonymous with wicked, cruel, and malicious behavior. She was Ahab's partner and wife. Ahab trivialized sin. He made it popular to worship the pagan god Baal, and he set up altars for the people to worship him. The worship of Baal was so hideous in its practice that it was closely associated with the worship of Molech, the child sacrifice god of the Old Testament.[2]

These were wicked times in Israel's history. The people had wandered away from God. They had forgotten his word and no longer obeyed his commands. The teachings of the world had crept into the minds and hearts of God's people. Wickedness was acceptable, and evil behavior ruled the day. If anyone felt guilty about their immoral actions, then all they needed to do was look to their king, Ahab, and their conscience would be appeased. Ahab and Jezebel popularized iniquity and promoted transgression. Jezebel even made it her practice to go around killing the prophets of God. This is the dark time in which Elijah was called to preach and to teach God's people.

God used Elijah to issue his judgment against Ahab and Israel by causing a severe drought that resulted in a famine. Elijah prophesied that there would be "neither dew nor rain in the next few years except at my word."[3] This did very little to turn Ahab's heart around, and the evil deeds and Baal worship increased throughout Israel.

Elijah, being a man of faith, decided to take action against the prophets of Baal. He made up his mind to do something about the false prophets, these wicked men leading God's people astray. There could be no room for doubt in Elijah's mind if he was going to take on King Ahab and the prophets of Baal, if he was going to have any chance of turning the hearts of God's people around.

Elijah gives us an incredible example of great faith. We can learn from his life and how godly faith is applied:

1. Go Public

Elijah's confrontation of the prophets of Baal is a great example of how someone acts when they are "sure of what they hope for and certain of what they do not see." Elijah summoned all the people of Israel together and also called all the prophets of Baal together, all 450 of them, along with 400 prophets of Asherah.[4]

The first action of someone who has faith and is to go public. So many times, we want to see the result of our faith, but we keep what we "hope for" all to ourselves. We are afraid to go public with what we believe will happen. We worry about how we will look; we're afraid of what "they" will say. What will people think? Even the most religious people sometimes scoff at true faith. In our silence, doubt starts to creep into our hearts. We don't go public with our plans. We hold back on proclaiming what we hope for just in case it doesn't happen. We don't want to be embarrassed, we don't want to look like a fool, so we keep our dreams, our prayers and our hopes to ourselves.

Not Elijah. You can imagine the scene: Word goes out throughout Israel that Elijah wants everyone to assemble at Mount Carmel, along with all the prophets of Baal. There was no second-guessing in Elijah's heart; there was no back door plan for him to run through. He was going public in a big way. Ahab wanted Elijah dead, and Elijah was exposing himself to all of Israel. If we are "sure of what we hope for," then we don't have an exit strategy. We don't have a back door to escape through in case things go wrong, because we are sure of what will happen.

You can imagine the scene as everyone assembled. There was a buzz in the air. People wanted to get a glimpse of Elijah because they'd heard about him, but you can imagine that few wanted to risk associating with him. The people talked, whispering among themselves. Everyone was speculating about what was going to happen. They studied Elijah, trying to figure him out. What did the crazy prophet have up his sleeve? You have to wonder what Elijah looked like at this point. I imagine him being calm and confident as he waited for everyone to assemble. It doesn't say how long it took for everyone to get there, but it didn't matter. Elijah's faith didn't waver over time. There was no worry in his heart. He was at peace. When we have true faith, there is no worry or anxiety. We are sure. All things are in God's hands, and we are at peace. Elijah waited for everyone to arrive. He didn't mind the audience because he was sure of what he was hoping for. He had no fear of being let down. He was going public in a big way.

If you want to begin to put great faith into practice, go public with your hopes— share your dreams with someone. Speak them aloud.

2. Walk the Talk

After Elijah assembled the people of Israel and the 850 prophets, he challenged the Israelites to choose: "How long will you waver between two opinions? If the LORD is God, follow him; but if Baal is God, follow him."[5]

Elijah knew that God was going to do something great, and he wanted those who were going to be with him to come forward. He was so sure of what was going to happen that he invited others along as witnesses. Elijah's actions show that he presumed a miracle from God was going to happen. He was absolutely sure of it, and prepared for it in advance. Elijah had no fear of failure. He had no fear that God might not answer his prayer. He was walking his talk. He didn't just sound like a faithful man, he acted like one. His actions showed that he was preparing for God's answer.

Let me ask you: After you pray for something, do you proceed as if it is already done? Do you go out knowing that God has heard your prayers, and then act accordingly? Faith is action. Faith is being sure. Faith is being certain. Elijah was certain that God was going to perform the miracle that day to turn Israel's heart back to him, and Elijah was preparing for it. He wasn't just hoping it would happen. He didn't wish that God would perform the miracle, he was certain of what he hoped for.

Elijah told the people:

> *"Get two bulls for us. Let them choose one for themselves, and let them cut it into pieces and put it on the wood but not set fire to it. I will prepare the other bull and put it on the wood but not set fire to it. Then you call on the name of your god, and I will call on the name of the LORD. The god who answers by fire—he is God."*
>
> *Then all the people said, "What you say is good."*
>
> *(1 Kings 18:23–24)*

You can see that Elijah had assembled the people so that he could put the prophets of Baal to the test publicly. He assembled the people so the prophets of Baal couldn't back down from his challenge. Elijah didn't allow himself a back door, and he wasn't going to allow a back door for the prophets of Baal. Elijah was absolutely certain that God would answer his prayer, and he acted accordingly. The prophets of Baal had no choice but to accept his challenge. If Elijah had any doubt in his heart, he would not have assembled all of Israel to witness this showdown.

The prophets of Baal began to call on Baal to bring down fire and burn up the sacrifice. They began in the morning and went through noon. They shouted and danced and cried out, but received no answer. At noon, Elijah began to taunt them. You can hear the confidence in his comments. Elijah's faith was on display. It is easy to have confidence after the fact, but Elijah had it before a miracle ever occurred. If Elijah had gone first and seen the miracle of God already happen, then it would be easy to understand his taunting the prophets of Asherah and Baal, but Elijah hadn't stepped forward yet. He was still on deck! However, he continued his taunting. He told them, "Shout louder! Surely he is a god! Perhaps he's deep in thought, or busy, or traveling" (v27). Actually, a more accurate translation for "maybe he's busy" would be, "Maybe your god isn't answering you because he's in the bathroom." The whole time Israel was watching this, they must have been thinking, "Elijah, you're next." This went on until evening, and there was no response from Baal.

So Elijah called the people to him. He had them repair the altar and make it ready for the sacrifice, but then he said,

> *"Fill four large jars with water and pour it on the offering and on the wood."*
>
> *"Do it again," he said, and they did it again.*
>
> *"Do it a third time," he ordered, and they did it the third time. The water ran down around the altar and even filled the trench.*
>
> *(vv33–35)*

Elijah made it abundantly clear to everyone. This altar would not catch fire by some strange circumstance or trickery. The wood, the ground and the sacrifice were soaking wet. This was so the people couldn't say that Elijah had done it by some sleight of hand or illusion. This was to demonstrate the power of God, and Elijah's faith was on display.

Let me ask you: When has your faith been on display? When have you stepped forward to "walk your talk?" When have you been so certain that something you prayed for was going to happen that you were absolutely sure of the results before anything ever happened?

It's time to start walking in the direction of what you hope for!

3. Don't Be Surprised

Then Elijah stepped forward and prayed,

"O LORD, God of Abraham, Isaac and Israel, let it be known today that you are God in Israel and that I am your servant and have done all these things at your command. Answer me, O LORD, answer me, so these people will know that you, O LORD, are God, and that you are turning their hearts back again."

Then the fire of the LORD fell and burned up the sacrifice, the wood, the stones and the soil, and also licked up the water in the trench.

When all the people saw this, they fell prostrate and cried, "The LORD—he is God! The LORD—he is God!" (vv36–39)

Elijah's prayer was answered. God sent down the fire from above and burned up everything on the altar, including the stones and the soil. There was no doubt about it. God sent a message to Israel that day. He showed the people that he was God. There is none other like him.

God answered Elijah's prayer, and the people fell down and worshiped God. The only one who wasn't surprised was Elijah. He knew that God would perform this miracle that day. I believe he was grateful and awed by the power of God, but he wasn't surprised. He had prepared for this to happen, he assembled the people to witness it, and he was even prepared to command the Israelites to seize the wicked prophets. Elijah wasn't surprised because his faith had already seen the sacrifice burn. That day Elijah's faith turned the people's hearts back to God, and his example was so powerful that it still speaks to us today.

We shouldn't be surprised when we see God working in our lives. Jesus tells us, "If you believe, you will receive whatever you ask for in prayer."[6] When we receive things from God, we should be abundantly grateful and praise his name, but we shouldn't be surprised.

"Elijah was a man just like us."[7] If we were to go back in time and meet Elijah, you would notice that, except for his clothes, he was just like us! He was a normal human being, but we have to know that the same power that was available to him is available to us today. Our hopes and dreams cannot just be something we wish for. Let's have the faith to share our dreams with others, then walk our own talk and act boldly on our faith, then stand back ready to praise God as his miracles unfold!

The Certain Three

If you do not stand firm in your faith, you will not stand at all.

–Isaiah 7:9

We *should* have faith, we *should* be certain—but sometimes we aren't. Life hits us hard, or maybe it just catches us by surprise. We want to be faithful, we long to believe, but we don't feel absolutely sure. Time is ticking and our faith is challenged, and we feel stuck. Ironically, it's usually the smaller daily struggles that can challenge our faithfulness the most.

One night I was trying desperately to make it to the Pudong Airport in Shanghai, China, so I could arrive home in Hong Kong to see my wife and four children later that evening. Only one more flight was scheduled to depart that night, and unless I wanted to spend the night in Shanghai, I needed to be on that plane. My business partner helped me catch a taxi and instructed the taxi driver, in Mandarin Chinese, to "step on it," because by all appearances there was no way I could make it to the airport on time. For added measure, everyone I worked with that evening offered their "encouragement," saying, "You're never going to make it."

Wanting to be a man of faith, I asked God to help me catch my flight, and set my mind to being *sure* and *certain* that we would make it on time. I wanted to apply my faith, not just say the prayer, so I decided to conduct myself as someone who was going to catch my flight. I sat back in my seat, relaxed in the taxi, and stopped checking my watch every ten seconds. I concentrated on banishing worry from my mind, and set my heart to be sure that God would come through. I told myself that there was nothing I could do at this point except surrender to God's plan. Judging by the way the taxi driver was barreling down the highway, my life was in God's hands anyway.

I was feeling pretty calm—and proud of my little victory—when my phone rang. My eleven-year-old daughter was on the line, asking in her sweet voice, "Daddy, will you be home tonight? Do you remember that I have a recital tomorrow morning? You promised you would come!" My heart skipped a beat.

I felt stuck, and at that moment, I knew my faith still needed to grow. I know that I can handle the possible disappointment of an unanswered prayer. I understand that God is sovereign, and he is in control of all things. I would not whine or fall into unbelief simply because of a missed flight. I firmly believe that God has reasons for what he does, and I will faithfully submit to his plan, not mine. However, when you throw my daughter's young faith and her feelings into the mix…that's a different story. How could I tell her to pray for me to make my flight, and expose her to the possible disappointment of not seeing her prayer answered? How could I teach her about faith in the almighty God if I missed my flight? Could this turn into a victory for the enemy of our faith? For a moment, I was tempted to prepare my daughter for disappointment, but I had decided to trust God, so I renewed my promise to her that I wouldn't miss my flight—after all, if I was sure of God's help, then I could make that guarantee.

Just when we think we have faith, it gets challenged even more. Then we have decisions to make. Will we start spiraling downward? It's funny, but sometimes Christians use events like catching a flight to define God's love for them. ("If I miss my flight, that means God doesn't care about me.") How wrong that thinking is! God's love for us was defined at the cross.

As I hurtled down that Chinese highway on a Friday night, I desperately wanted to catch my flight. I asked my daughter to pray for me. I continued to conduct myself in the surest way I knew how, but still I heard that little voice, that little twinge in the back of my head that wanted to prepare for disappointment. That's the way of the world: Expect the worst, then you'll never be let down. It's safer not to have faith at all. Don't put your trust in God, only to be disillusioned or disappointed.

It is here that we can learn a powerful lesson from "the three amigos" of the Bible: Shadrach, Meshach, and Abednego. As the story goes, King Nebuchadnezzar built a statue of gold ninety feet high and nine feet wide, and when he dedicated it, he proclaimed that whenever music was played, all people of every nation and every language were to fall down and worship the statue. Anyone who did not fall down and worship would be immediately thrown into a blazing furnace. Shadrach, Meshach, and Abednego, who were faithful men of God, refused to bow down to the image of gold. When they were confronted and arrested, they exclaimed,

> *"O Nebuchadnezzar, we do not need to defend ourselves before you in this matter. If we are thrown into the blazing furnace, the God we serve is able to save us from it, and he will rescue us from your hand, O king. But even if he does not, we want you to know, O king, that we will not serve your gods or worship the image of gold you have set up."*
>
> *(Daniel 3:16–18)*

We can learn a glorious lesson from these three great men of faith: Their faith allowed them to say, "But even if he does not..." They told Nebuchadnezzar that it didn't matter if God chose not to save them that day. They were still going to do what was right. They weren't going to bow down to serve another god. Their faith would remain in the one true God no matter whether he saved them that day or not.

Is your faith strong enough to say that? Does your faith allow God to work as he pleases? Shadrach, Meshach, and Abednego had already decided that the outcome didn't matter, their faith was firm and secure. If God chose to take their lives that day in the fiery furnace after they had made their public profession of faith, they would not waver through unbelief. They were choosing to be righteous, rejecting the ways of the world, refusing to bow down and worship another god, choosing to worship the one true God. Even if God chose not to save them that day, they were going to be faithful to him.

Have a faith that allows God to work as he sees fit, a faith that allows his will to be done, that doesn't waver through unbelief. True faith means that we can say, "I trust God and his plan, even if he chooses not to answer my prayer." True faith still honors and obeys him, even when we don't get our way. True faith glorifies him as God because he can do as he decides.

God is worthy of our total belief, whatever he decides for us: "In his heart a man plans his course, but the LORD determines his steps."[1] This is what we need to live and teach our children. No matter the outcome, we will serve God. Our faith is not a formula for getting what we want; our faith is an unwavering certainty in the almighty God!

Oh and by the way, I made my flight.

Part III

ADD TO YOUR FAITH

"…Make every effort to add to your faith…"
- 2 Peter 1:5

71

The Goal of Grace

*Like newborn babies, crave pure spiritual milk, so that by it
you may grow up in your salvation.*

—1 Peter 2:2

At this point, our internal battle for faith may begin to get us tangled
up, because we want to believe and be sure, but we find conundrums
at every turn. How can I say that we are to believe and not doubt,
but then urge you to accept the fact that sometimes God may say no?
Are we really supposed to have absolute confidence that our every
prayer will be answered yes, or are we supposed to have faith in the
overarching truths of who God is—his power, presence, wisdom,
and will? How does this life of certainty fit into the prayers of a
married couple who have been longing for years to have a child,
the prayers of a single sister who wants to get married someday, the
pleas of a dad with cancer, the parents' requests for their child with
a learning disorder? Are we to live with the certainty that God will
fix everything, or are we to accept life as it is?

The best way I can answer that is to look in the Bible. Let's
look at a man whose faith was far ahead of ours: David. Remember
the time when David really messed up ("messed up" is a profound
understatement)? He slept with a married woman, and when

she got pregnant, David had her husband killed to cover it up.[1] Remember, this is the same David that God called "a man after his own heart."[2]

The story continues in 2 Samuel 12. After Nathan prophesied that the son born to David and Bathsheba would die, the Bible says,

After Nathan had gone home, the LORD struck the child that Uriah's wife had borne to David, and he became ill. David pleaded with God for the child. He fasted and went into his house and spent the nights on the ground. (2 Samuel 12:15–16).

David desperately wanted to save the life of his son. He fasted, prayed, and slept on the ground for seven days. David was desperately making his appeal to God. He urgently wanted God to hear his prayers and answer. No one would argue that David was not one of the most faithful men who ever lived. He lived a life with complete confidence in God, and witnessed God's blessings all the time; however, after seven days of fasting and praying, the child that had been born to David and Bathsheba died, and the Scripture says,

David's servants were afraid to tell him that the child was dead, for they thought, "While the child was still living, we spoke to David but he would not listen to us. How can we tell him the child is dead? He may do something desperate." (2 Samuel 12:18)

Here's our answer. The servants thought that David would do something crazy after he found out that the child had died. They thought he would be mad at God and take out his anger in some extreme way, but when David realized that the child was dead, the Bible says,

Then David got up from the ground. After he had washed, put on lotions and changed his clothes, he went into the house of the LORD and worshiped. (2 Samuel 12:20)

David didn't spend the next couple weeks moaning and groaning and doubting God's existence or his goodness because things didn't turn out the way he prayed. He accepted God's answer and praised God even through his heartache.

I believe that God's answer to David's prayer—"no"—served as a reminder to David for the rest of his life, a reminder that God wasn't finished with him. God was still working on him to help him grow and change. It was a reminder of his sin, and a reminder of how quickly David could forget his God and go astray.

Let me ask you: Have you ever seen a football player point to the sky after he scores a touchdown? We all think, "Oh, wow, he believes in God." I believe the truly faithful man is the one who, after dropping the touchdown pass, points to the sky as if to say, "I'm learning and growing, because God has a bigger purpose for me."

I can remember a time, years ago, when I was out looking for work. I had reached a point that I was willing to accept any job that came along, but it seemed that the answer was always "no." Interview after interview, I was told "no," and I became very discouraged, thinking that things would never turn out the way I had hoped. I found it hard to find the motivation to continue looking for a job, thinking that all my efforts were useless. Then something changed. My circumstances didn't change—*I* changed. I decided to enjoy the interview process and try my best to learn from every situation. I would try my very best to improve after each interview (which sometimes felt more like an interrogation!). I decided to listen and learn, and at the end of each interview I began asking the interviewer, "What was something that I could have done better in this interview?"

I soon found myself interviewing for a job that I desperately wanted, working for Fisher-Price toy company. I never would have been prepared for this one interview had I not gone through all those other interviews. I got the job, and I believe I got it because of what I had gone through during all those long months of disappointment, when I learned how to answer tough interview questions. Had I not experienced those other *failures,* I don't think I would have gotten the job I truly wanted. After I finally got my dream job, I realized that my previous efforts were not failures at all—they were necessary steps that God used to prepare me for what he had in store for me!

If there is one verse in the Bible that sums up almost the entire New Testament, it is Hebrews 10:14: "...by one sacrifice he has made perfect forever those who are being made holy." This one verse can help to explain our spiritual dilemmas with faith and set us on the right course.

We were made perfect forever by the one sacrifice of Jesus, but becoming holy is a continual process. That bears repeating: We were made perfect forever by the one sacrifice of Jesus, but becoming holy is a continual process. God and his Spirit are engaged in an ongoing effort to draw us out of the world, out of worldly thinking and worldly pursuits, to help us become more like Christ—more spiritual, more godly, more holy. God not only uses our victories, but also our difficulties, struggles, and defeats. All of these experiences are intended to help us become more like Christ.

There is a vast difference between becoming more spiritual and becoming more religious. When you think of someone becoming more spiritual, do you also envision that person becoming more faithful? Don't faithfulness and holiness go hand in hand? They work together. As we grow in our holiness, we should also grow in our faithfulness, as faith is an essential part of our holiness. However, when you think of a religious person, what do you picture? I picture someone handing out flyers, going to church, and using God's name in conversations, but does that really mean the person is living a faithful life and that their life is being made holy? Not necessarily. The goal of Christianity is not to become more religious and just do a bunch of religious things, but the goal of Christianity is to become more holy, more Christlike. We can only grow in this way because we have been made perfect by that one sacrifice of Jesus.

I once met an old Jewish man. He was a stamp collector and had many years of experience collecting stamps. I had found some old stamps and brought them to him to get his assessment of their value. While he examined the stamps, we started to talk about God. We seemed to agree on the same God, the one true God. Then he removed his thick glasses and said, "Yes, but what I want to know is, if God were to come down to earth and visit us, where would he go? What would he say? Who would he hang out with? What would his day be like? Essentially, what would God be like? This would be fascinating to know."

My response, without even giving it much thought, was, "That's Jesus." My answer seemed to startle him, and we weren't able to pick up our conversation after that.

Jesus is the completion of our faith. He is perfect, and he made us perfect by his sacrifice, but we must continue to strive to be like him. Now that we have faith, we must grow in our faith to become more of who God wants us to be. The goal was never to just have faith and then stop—the goal is to become like his son. God sent Jesus as our perfect example of living a godly life, and it is only by God's continual grace and love for us that we can live to fight another day to be like him. We live each day to become like him.

As 2 Peter 1:3-8 puts it,

His divine power has given us everything we need for life and godliness through our knowledge of him who called us by his own glory and goodness. Through these he has given us his very great and precious promises, so that through them you may participate in the divine nature and escape the corruption in the world caused by evil desires.

For this very reason, make every effort to add to your faith goodness; and to goodness, knowledge; and to knowledge, self-control; and to self-control, perseverance; and to perseverance, godliness; and to godliness, brotherly kindness; and to brotherly kindness, love. For if you posses these qualities in increasing measure, they will keep you from being ineffective and unproductive in your knowledge of our Lord Jesus Christ.

The goal is to *add* to our faith so that we will *grow* in our faith. If we stop growing, then we become unproductive religious people following a bunch of rules—hardly a lifestyle that inspires a watching world! If we grow in our holiness, then we can truly be a light to the world.

The remarkable thing is that Jesus laid out an amazing plan for us in some of the very first words he ever preached. He described for us the direction we should be heading every day. In the introduction to that famous sermon—just a few lines of written text—he changed the course of humanity and laid the foundation for our Christianity. His teachings are summarized in the eloquent and concise beatitudes. The first seven are paradoxes, and the eighth describes the result of following the others.

Let's explore each of them together and look into the purpose, direction, and practical daily application for our faith as we live on a world the size of a cue ball, held in the palm of God's glorious hand.

Pursue Poverty

Blessed are the poor in spirit, for theirs is the kingdom of heaven.

— Matthew 5:3

It's not something that we want to admit, but we spend most of our lives working for financial security. We desperately work to obtain a secure place in this life. We go to school hoping to get the best job so we can make enough money to pay the bills, own a home, put money away for our kids' college, and eventually retire.

I remember attending a financial seminar not too long ago where the speaker was discussing saving up for retirement. He explained how to maximize contributions to our 401(k). He demonstrated how, if you start contributing to a 401(k) in your early twenties, by the time you are forty, you will have put aside enough money for retirement and you can then stop contributing to your 401(k). The fund will continue to grow even without additional contributions, as the interest on your investment will compound and your money will continue to grow. He showed a chart of how the investment would look over time. There was a nice clean slope heading upwards over time as the money continued to work for itself and grow nicely. Then, he showed an example of someone who starts contributing to their

401(k) in their late thirties or early forties. Even if they contribute longer than the person who starts in their twenties, their investment will never catch up to the person who began contributing earlier and then stopped contributing. At that point, you could look around the room and see our faces, each of us echoing a silent "Yikes!"

We all have a basic fear. It is near the top of the list of people's biggest fears, along with public speaking and death—it's the fear of poverty. We all desperately want to avoid poverty at all costs. We work ourselves to the bone, trying to avoid destitution and promote our own security. People have been known to do some crazy things to ensure their own financial stability.

Some of the very first words Jesus ever spoke in public were his pronunciation, "Blessed are the poor in spirit, for theirs is the kingdom of heaven." It is no surprise that people began to plot Jesus' death shortly thereafter!

When Jesus came to earth, the light dawned on mankind; but light can be painful to let in. We don't want the light in the morning, after resting in darkness for so long. The light hurts, so we hit the snooze alarm. John the Baptist tried to prepare everyone for the shocking light Jesus would usher into the world, but we were still not ready to hear him. The darkness in our hearts has a hard time grasping Jesus' very first teaching, "Blessed are the poor in spirit," but those who want to live a life of faith must embrace this teaching.

Before we can start to understand what Jesus is teaching us, we should begin by establishing what he is not teaching. There is a way to be "poor in spirit" that is different from the blessed state that Jesus is speaking of, a mindset that is far removed from the happiness and joy Jesus wants us to have. It can be called false humility. False humility can resemble being poor in spirit, yet it is really only out for selfish gain and worldly ambition.

Someone with false humility will pretend to be poor in spirit and show signs of humility, but they are only modifying their outward behavior. They have enough sense to know that pride is of no value. It doesn't get them what they want, yet inwardly their heart rages with arrogance and conceit. False humility is easy to spot because it becomes obvious when a person's position or standing is challenged.

Their inward pride will expose itself. When someone is truly serving the Lord as a humble servant, they are not threatened when others take up the desire to serve; they welcome the help because the workload is spread out. However, someone with false humility will feel threatened by others doing the work. They tend to be driven for their own gain, their own success.

Being poor in spirit can be summed up by three key qualities that work in union with each other: emptying ourselves of worldliness, knowing who God is, and having a true inner humility. We will break down each of these qualities and describe them in more detail.

Empty Yourself of Worldliness

We are all like a container that is already full of something, but God has plans for us to be used for a different purpose. Our container must first be emptied of its old contents to make room for the new. When we empty ourselves of worldliness, there is now room for godliness. Once the worldliness is gone, we are free to develop a gracious and humble nature of the soul. We must be completely emptied first of our *self*: our selfish ambitions, worldly pursuits, and worldly passions. Only then do we have room for God to fill us up.

For most of us, this is a very challenging task, as our worldly pursuits describe and define us. They become both our labels and our identity. We are lawyers, doctors, managers, athletes, students, mothers, fathers; we are healthy, smart, funny, considerate, energetic...fill in the blank. The list of labels is infinite, but the older we get, the more of them we acquire, and the more permanent they can become. Our carefully crafted personas tell the world who we are—everything from the clothes we wear and the houses we own, to the business cards we hand out. We spend years honing an image for ourselves, and the image we want to present to the world.

Our labels and worldly definitions have no value for where we are going after this life. Ecclesiastes 9:4 says, "Anyone who is among the living has hope—even a live dog is better off than a dead lion!" In this life, we could be considered the smartest, strongest, fastest, or richest, but from God's perspective, it doesn't matter how you are perceived by the world or what your business card says. To God, there is only one label that will matter in the end: Christian. We are to empty ourselves of everything else that fills us up.

Many people may not feel that they have an impressive label to begin with, or they may view themselves as being in a poor condition already, but that does not mean they are necessarily poor in spirit. They mope around because of their predicament in life, sharing their complaints freely with anyone who will listen, but still they are not poor in spirit. They remain proud. It's like the guy who is unhappy that he cannot get a job. He is down and out, but he refuses to cut his hair for a job interview because he doesn't want anyone to tell him what to do. Or it's like the woman who is discouraged that she has no true friendships, but is not willing to listen to others' thoughts and opinions. She has a sharp comment for everything, but is not aware that conversation is fifty-fifty. It's funny how people in situations like this can lack the humility appropriate to their circumstances. They should be humble, but they can't seem to find humility even when humility is obviously the best and wisest choice.

People who are poor in spirit will accept the lot that God has given them in life. They recognize that God is sovereign over the world, and he gives and takes as he sees fit. If God has appointed us to worldly poverty today, then we surrender to his wisdom, but at the same time, we still retain the ability to be grateful for what we do have.

We should not cast off or throw aside the things that God has given, nor should we treat them with contempt or disdain. Some people live feeling guilty for what they do have; others feel discontent because of what they don't have. We should not throw away what God has given us, nor should we look down on others who may posses more (or less) than we do. 1 Timothy 6:6 says, "But godliness with contentment is great gain." We need nothing else in this world but to be godly. That should be enough for us, and it all begins with being poor in spirit, having a humble heart that is emptied of all its worldly pursuits.

We know we are emptying ourselves of worldly ambitions when we begin to place greater value on godliness than on worldliness.

For example, as a parent, is it more important that your daughter becomes the star on her soccer team, or that she fears God and reads her Bible every day? Is it more important that your son never misses a baseball practice, or never misses a Bible Talk? Dads, do you teach your kids more about giving their all in the classroom or giving their all to God? Do we stress the importance of committing to a team, but fail to teach commitment to God? Have I worked hard to win the acceptance and praise of my boss and coworkers, but fallen short in winning the approval of God? What we value in life will tell us if we have emptied ourselves of our worldly pursuits or not.

God Is God and We Are Not

The second part of being poor in spirit is to acknowledge that God is great—far greater than anything we can possibly comprehend. I know that sounds simple, but does it go down into the core of our being? As we go to God in prayer, and as we approach him in faith, we must have a completely surrendered attitude, recognizing the magnitude and glory of the almighty God. Only then can we recognize our own poor and lowly position. This has to be the truth from which all of our actions, speech, and motives originate—that God is great and we are not.

Our faith and knowledge of God should not allow us to approach him with any sense of entitlement. Our spirit, when we go to God, should be like that of a beggar in the streets, one with his hand out for God's grace and mercy. God is the wealthy person stopping to help the homeless. We approach God in utter humility, hoping and praying that he will notice us and give us the grace that we so urgently need. When God hears us and answers our prayers, he is showing us his grace. It is humbling to know that God's gifts of life and breath are gifts of grace, and yet he blesses us with so much more: our families, the church, his word, his Spirit, his mercy. Our standing in this life does not matter; we approach God knowing that every crumb he gives us is a blessing. Although he treats us as sons and daughters, we approach God knowing that he is completely holy and we are utterly sinful. To be poor in spirit is to go to God with complete reverence and awe, in both fear and wonder.

Jesus said, "How hard it is for the rich to enter the kingdom of God!"[1] The rich can easily lose touch with their desperate need for God. When their wealth can provide all the comfort they think they need, then how can they see their need for God? Listen to what Jesus tells the church in Laodicea:

"You say, 'I am rich; I have acquired wealth and do not need a thing.' But you do not realize that you are wretched, pitiful, poor, blind and naked." (Revelation 3:17)

Look at the huge disparity between the way the Laodiceans viewed themselves and the way Jesus viewed them. They thought of themselves as rich and needing nothing, yet Jesus thought of them as poor and in desperate need. They thought of themselves as successful and self-sufficient, but Jesus saw them as wretched, pitiful, poor, blind and naked. Their wealth couldn't cover the nakedness that they were exposing to God. They had lost touch with truly being in want and need. They did not want anything anymore. They felt fine. They were no longer desperate.

The problem begins with how we see ourselves. Have we lost touch with what we truly need spiritually—that our needs are not of this world, nor could they be satisfied by the world? We should long to be rich—but rich in faith, hope, and love. We need from God "the treasures of wisdom and knowledge."[2] These treasures are not hidden from us, beyond our ability to grasp. We need from God the things that will make our souls rich. Although the Laodiceans were proud of themselves, they should have been pitied. Although Jesus had told them to be poor in spirit, they had become swollen with pride.

When you go to God in prayer, are you proud in your spirit? To be proud in spirit does not mean that we necessarily say proud things—pride exists in our hearts and is evident in the manner in which we approach God. If we rarely go to God in prayer, we are proud. By not asking, by not begging, by not crying out to God, we communicate to him that we are just fine and don't need anything. Does your lack of humble prayer say to God that you think you are okay? When was the last time you prayed on your knees? When was the last time you were on your face in prayer? Does this only happen when circumstance drives you to your knees, down on your face, or do you have this posture in prayer when life is good, just to praise God and thank him?

When the church in Laodicea thought they were rich, they were really poor. Had they only realized their spiritual poverty, they could have become truly rich with eternal treasure.

Humility Begins Within

The third key to being poor in spirit is looking humbly into the mirror at ourselves, rather than constantly building ourselves up in our own minds and hearts, always thinking we are something. A poor spirit begins within. Our humility must start on the inside.

A great test of our inward humility is when we hear that someone else has fallen on hard times or is struggling through circumstances. If we secretly rejoice, thinking that their misfortune may improve our position in life, we are proud and we value the wrong things. We should imitate Paul's attitude: He considered himself "the least of all the apostles."[3] He saw himself as "less than the least of all God's people."[4] He valued all other people above himself.

To be poor in spirit, we must value others more than we value ourselves. We must surrender ourselves to the needs of others. How do we do this? We first think of the other person before we think of ourselves. When you are in a room with someone, do you consider their needs first? Are you quick to listen to what they have to say? Are you willing to get up to greet them and make them feel welcome? Are they hungry, thirsty, in need of some rest? How are things going with their family, job, health, their wife, husband, and children? How are they faring emotionally, mentally, physically, and spiritually? When you speak to people, do you make them feel as if they are the only person in the room, that they have your complete attention—or do you have so much on your mind that you can't focus on anyone else, you're just waiting for the conversation to come around to you? Do people feel like you sympathize and understand them? That you truly and deeply care?

When you are poor in spirit, you give yourself wholly to others and have a genuine concern that radiates in every conversation. After someone spends time with you, they feel encouraged and inspired. They feel loved and important. This is the spirit of Jesus coming through you.

Our society resists this attitude because it appears weak in its thinking. From a very early age our kids are told, "You can't just let people walk all over you; you can't just be a doormat. If you don't watch out for yourself, no one else will. Love yourself. Take care of yourself first."

Jesus came with a radical doctrine, one that the world still cannot embrace. If we look out for others, Jesus promises that he will look out for us.

Jesus assures that those who surrender themselves to this poverty of soul will be happy. He asks us to dig deep into our hearts and empty ourselves of our worldly pursuits; to go to God in desperate need, recognizing our lowly state, and to consider others better than ourselves. When we do all this, Jesus can begin to display his power in us. If we trust in God to lay this foundation deep within us, then we will truly be happy.

Mourn Continually

Blessed are those who mourn, for they will be comforted.
—Matthew 5:4

As Jesus continues the Sermon on the Mount, the irony of his words becomes even more pronounced. Jesus declares that we will be blessed if we mourn, and happy if we are sad. If we are honest, most of us have never thought of adding the idea of mourning to our faith, but Jesus says that mourning is absolutely vital for a Christian's existence on this earth, and that in the end, it will bring comfort. We know that God's plan for us is that someday when we are in heaven,

> *"He will wipe every tear from their eyes. There will be no more death or mourning or crying or pain, for the old order of things has passed away." (Revelation 21:4)*

When we make it to heaven, there will be no more mourning; there will be no more pain. God will finally be with his people, and his people will finally be with their God. Everything will be made new. As God was in the beginning, so he will be in the end. We will finally enter the heavenly city. Our eternal life will begin. The time spent in this world will have been but a blink of the eye compared to eternity with God. We will have no use for tears in heaven, and all sadness will disappear.

So, how is it that a Christian's faith could be happier, more complete if we mourn? Why does Jesus call Christians to mourn? Once again, we first have to understand what Jesus is *not* teaching us. There is a mourning that does not qualify us for God's blessing. It is a worldly mourning. It is a sorrow that comes from the devil, and it is when we mourn for what we do not have. It is self-pity—the sorrow that comes from not getting what you believe you deserve. It is a sadness that comes from a long life of working hard, but not getting the results that we had hoped for. It is the mourning that eventually turns to bitterness. It is a sadness that may remain under the surface of the image we present to the world, but that permeates our thinking and sours our hearts. Inwardly, we feel robbed by life, because it wasn't supposed to be like this.

You can see this attitude in the older brother in Jesus' parable of the prodigal son. When the repentant son returns home and his father throws a party to celebrate his return, the older brother—the brother who stayed home and always obeyed his father—is angry. His resentment finally boils over when he says,

> *"Look! All these years I've been slaving for you and never disobeyed your orders. Yet you never gave me even a young goat so I could celebrate with my friends." (Luke 15:29)*

The truth finally spills out. He is mad and jealous. He feels that he is due something from his father. The father owes him for all his years of service, and he had thought his day was coming, especially after his younger brother went off and squandered his inheritance. Surely, the older brother would now receive his due.

The problem is that he doesn't understand his father. He doesn't understand the love his father has for his children. It's not about getting in line; it's not about receiving our due. It's about being with the Father. Everything is available to those who are with the Father.

Are we content with what God has given us, or do we long for more—or even feel that we deserve more? Do we secretly wish we had more money, more prestige, more respect, more power? Even if

God gave us these things, would we glorify him with the money, prestige, respect, and power—or are we like the older brother, who just wanted it so he could go celebrate with his friends? This is not the kind of self-centered, worldly mourning that Jesus wants from us.

Consider King David, the king of Israel, the brave warrior. The one who faced Goliath, inspiring the women to sing, "He has slain his tens of thousands."[1] He was mighty indeed! However, David was also the one who said:

> *Be merciful to me, LORD, for I am faint;*
>   *O LORD, heal me, for my bones are in agony.*
> *My soul is in anguish.*
>   *How long, O LORD, how long?*
> *Turn, O LORD, and deliver me;*
>   *save me because of your unfailing love.*
> *No one remembers you when he is dead.*
>   *Who praises you from the grave?*
>
> *I am worn out from groaning;*
>   *all night long I flood my bed with weeping*
> *and drench my couch with tears.*
>   *My eyes grow week with sorrow;*
> *they fail because of all my foes.*
>
> *Away from me, all you who do evil,*
>   *for the LORD has heard my weeping.*
> *The LORD has heard my cry for mercy;*
>   *the LORD accepts my prayer.*
> *(Psalm 6:2–9)*

In another Psalm he said,

> *Streams of tears flow from my eyes,*
>   *for your law is not obeyed.*
> *(Psalm 119:136)*

David had something in his relationship with God, something that many of us overlook. He had passion. David poured out his heart to God. He moved God by his tears, but most important, David was moved to tears himself because God's laws were not being obeyed.

Men in David's life were unjust and corrupt. Their sin and betrayals pained him. He wept—not only because of his own suffering, but because God was dishonored by their actions. He felt the same way God feels when men disobey: He grieved over their sin.

Do you grieve at disobedience? When you sin against God, does it bring you to tears? When you hear of someone else's sin, does it make you sad? Do you weep when someone turns away from God? Do your tear ducts still work, or can you even remember the last time you cried? Even more important, can you remember the last time you cried because of sin in the world, the sin that is sending millions upon millions to hell?

Consider Jeremiah, the prophet who compared his eyes to "a fountain of tears" because of the sin that was in Jerusalem.[2] He felt physical pain over the sin of God's people. Not only had they become a sinful people, but they had even forgotten how to blush.[3] They had forgotten how to feel ashamed of their sin. They had grown numb to the commands of God. Their hearts had grown calloused and they didn't even know it.

I am constantly amazed by the things we sit down and watch on television, and by the movies we let into our homes. We sit with our children and watch films that the government says are inappropriate for kids, rating them with PG–13 or R, but we pop the popcorn, gather the family around, and watch the filth of the world with our children. Then, as if that weren't bad enough, we tell other Christians about it and *don't even blush!* We show no shame. Sometimes, even though we wouldn't trust the government to raise our kids, we even disregard the federal warnings that certain shows or movies "may be inappropriate" for children! We say, "'Peace, peace,'...when there is no peace."[4] The world isn't just creeping into our homes; we are holding the door open for it, gathering our families around it and applauding. I once heard a brother get up in front of a church and talk about a "good" movie that celebrated adultery, promoted envy and deceit, had many inappropriate sexual scenes, and literally glorified the devil. Somehow, he found a lesson in this movie that the church should learn from. That is ridiculous! Jesus tells us to have nothing to do with such evil.

When I am watching a movie with my family, I hold the remote in my hand the whole time. I keep one finger on the mute button and another poised to change channels in an instant. I believe I am doing three things when I change the channel during inappropriate scenes. One, I'm keeping the evil out of my home, out of my family, and out of our children's impressionable minds. Two, I am teaching my children that you can't just sit back and say, "It's entertainment." I'm teaching them not to be subject to the world. They can turn this stuff off. I'm teaching them exactly what is appropriate and what is not, and if I have to change the channel or hit the mute button too often in a short span of time, then the movie is out. It's not acceptable. Third, I want my family to know that our home is a safe place. They don't have to keep their guard up at home. As their father, I will do everything I know to protect them and keep our home a safe place.

Someone may say, "But your children won't know how to deal with the 'real' world." My first instinct is to take whatever movie that person doesn't want to give up, smash it into little pieces and make them eat it (see Exodus 32:1–20, where Moses did exactly that with the Israelites' golden calf), but I know that is not an acceptable form of discipline in the New Testament! Instead, I say that we have to guard our hearts at all costs. Being in the world never taught me anything about the world. It was only when I became a Christian that I began to see the principles of the world at work in our lives. I began to see the craftiness of Satan and what he is trying to do to all of us. He wants to make us go astray. He wants us to get off the path and head in the wrong direction.

When you see the world at work like this, does it sadden you? Does it hurt you in the gut? Have you ever cried about it, called out to God for help? Let's read an intense story in Ezekiel 9. God sends out six men, each with a deadly weapon in his hand, and one man with a writing kit. God says,

> *"Go throughout the city of Jerusalem and put a mark on the foreheads of those who grieve and lament over all the detestable things that are done in it."*
>
> *As I listened, he said to the others, "Follow him throughout the city and kill, without showing pity or compassion. Slaughter old men, young men and maidens, women and children, but do not touch anyone who has the mark. Begin at my sanctuary." So they began with the elders who were in front of the temple.*
>
> *Then he said to them, "Defile the temple and fill the courts with the slain. Go!" So they went out and began killing throughout the city.*
>
> *(Ezekiel 9:4–7)*

First, God sent out a man among his people and told him to put a mark on people. It is believed that the mark written on people's foreheads was a *taw,* the last letter of the Hebrew alphabet—the shape of a cross.[5] This mark was to be put on the foreheads of anyone who had grieved or lamented over the detestable things that were done in Jerusalem. This mark decided whether they would live or die. If they had grieved about Jerusalem's sin, then they would live. If they hadn't, they were cut down and killed.

What a powerful image for us today. The ones who lived were the ones who received the mark on their foreheads. They were spared because they were disgusted by the disobedience of God's people in the world. They couldn't stomach the sin that was going on. They were saddened by what they saw among their neighbors, friends, and family. They cried about it. They asked God for his strength so they wouldn't be dragged into it. They called out for God to rescue them from evil. They mourned, and because of this they were saved.

I remember a Christian woman my wife and I once knew who went through some very difficult times. She was married to a man who was less than admirable. He had a drug problem, cheated on her, and was unable to help raise their two children. She never knew if he was coming home that night or not. My wife and I spent two years counseling her and her husband, trying to get him to repent and be the man for the family that he was supposed to be. She hung in there with him as long as she could, but after he had been in and out of jail for a long time, she felt that it was over. We spent time counseling her through a very difficult divorce, and she finally made it though to the other side.

I can remember many times over the two year period being brought to tears for her and her children. It broke our hearts to see what her husband was putting her and her family through. There were a few times when I didn't know what else to do but pray and shed tears.

Some time had passed and she met a strong Christian man who is now her husband and father of her two children. Thanks be to God!

How about you? Have you ever wept intensely for someone you love when you have seen them go through a difficult time, or shed tears when they themselves have gone in the wrong direction, when you have seen them getting caught up in sin? Do you feel anything when you see the disobedience in the world or in the church? Have you ever cried for your own soul? If you lived in the days of Ezekiel, would there be a mark on your forehead? Would there be a mark on your heart?

Beg God that you can be someone who is able to mourn for this lost world. Ask God to soften your heart so that you can feel the way God feels. You will be amazed at the peace it will bring into your life. You will be blessed by God.

Tread 18 Lightly

Blessed are the meek, for they will inherit the earth.

– Matthew 5:5

You can see it every day. Just open the newspaper and it's full of examples: families are shattered, torn apart; jobs are lost, businesses destroyed; the jailhouse is full. It's not hard to look around the world and spot the consequences of people losing control of their emotions, flying off the handle in rage. Many are the culprits; countless more are the victims.

Jesus offers us another paradox to add to our faith: "Blessed are the meek, for they will inherit the earth." Once again, we see how our society has gone astray by not heeding the words of Jesus. The world tells us that you have to be almost hostile or belligerent if you want to make it. You have to climb over others to get ahead; it's a dog–eat–dog world out there. In my view, one of the most ridiculous reality TV shows is *The Apprentice*. Contestants compete in cutthroat business and marketing challenges in order to earn a position working for Donald Trump, and at the end of every show, Donald eliminates (and humiliates) another contestant by saying, "You're fired." I would argue that if the contestants were as ruthless in the *real* business world as they were on the show, they would surely be fired; but on the show, selfishness and competitiveness are rewarded. But the show makes its viewers think that success in the business world only comes when you adopt the motto "Every man for himself." Jesus would not have done well on this show, nor should anyone who claims to follow him! Jesus calls us to be meek.

The word *meek* is not necessarily an attractive word or an inspiring thought. When we watch our children growing up, do we dream they will grow up to become meek? Is meekness a trait we aspire to ourselves? If you were to make a list of someone's strengths and weaknesses, the word *meek* probably would not appear in the strength column. I have reviewed scores of résumés, but never have I seen the word *meek* on an applicant's résumé. When you write down your New Year's goals, have you ever written down the goal to "become meeker"?

Society paints a meek person as being somewhat malnourished and weak. The world has given us an image that is a cross between a starving child and a frail elderly person. In fact, if we are honest, most of us have a hard time with Jesus' encouragement to become meek; we don't like this aspect of our Christianity. We want to aim for greatness, not meekness. We would probably admit that we accept this as "part" of Jesus' teaching, but we have a very hard time embracing it—and yet Jesus tells us that the meek are happy. These are the ones who will find the blessings of God. They will inherit the earth.

On one of my first business trips to Asia, I traveled with my dad and brother. The three of us were running the family business together. We were headed to Hong Kong to explore the idea of restructuring our business to remain competitive in the world. We weren't exactly sure what we were going to do, but we knew that we needed to be leaner and more efficient.

We were planning a face–to–face meeting, after many years of long-distance business association, with a man named Sing. For years he had worked behind the scenes in our Hong Kong operations, making sure our business ran well and that we didn't have anything to worry about on that side of the world. Whenever we spoke to any of his employees, they all spoke very highly of him, with a great sense of respect. You could tell that they were happy working for him.

Sing had learned that we wanted to restructure our business for the future, and sent word suggesting that the four of us meet for a time to brainstorm and plan. We had heard stories of this man's great wealth, his business ventures and success, so we jumped at the chance to meet with him and pick his brain.

Sing sent us word to let us know that his driver would pick us up at our hotel later that evening for dinner and our meeting. I thought the arrangement was fitting—of course a man of Sing's stature would send his driver to pick us up, since he couldn't be bothered with the menial tasks of everyday life. I pictured myself taking my first ride in a limo and heading out to a fancy restaurant, where we could discourse on business philosophy.

With great anticipation, I joined my brother and father in the hotel lobby to wait for Sing's driver. Right on time, someone met us in the lobby. It was Sing's wife. She was going to escort us to their car. My anticipation grew as we headed to their car—what kind of limo would we be riding in? Sing's wife stopped beside a very plain Toyota minivan. I tried to mask my surprise. She held the door for us while we climbed in to sit on the one bench seat in the back of the van, and then she walked around to the front to sit beside Romeo, the driver. Romeo wasn't wearing a black suit with a black cap as I had expected. I was doing my best to wrap my brain all of this when I heard a voice from the floor in the back of the van, just behind our seat: "Hello, boys."

I turned around, and there on the floor, scrunched up next to the spare tire, was a five-foot-seven-inch, 130-pound Chinese man with thick glasses, dressed in a coat and tie. This was the great Sing.

Seemingly oblivious to our shock, Sing smiled and said, "I knew there wasn't enough room for all of us to sit up there, and I'm obviously the smallest, so I am in the back." He then proceeded to ask how we were, and if we were enjoying our stay. We tried our best to not look amazed as we answered his questions, looking back over our shoulders and down at the floor. We worked with Sing for many years after that day, and he always maintained the same posture of humility and meekness. He was always the last person to walk through a door, and he made sure everyone else was comfortable before he would ever take his seat.

Whenever I picture meekness, I envision Sing, squeezed into the back of a minivan next to the spare tire so that his guests might be more comfortable. Sing is one of the meekest people I have ever met, and yet he earned more respect than anyone I have ever met. He had power and position, but carried himself humbly and gently. If you were not paying attention when you first met him, there's a good chance you could just dismiss him.

The meek are those who quietly surrender themselves to God and his dominion, power and rule. They submit themselves to his word and to his sovereignty. They accept his discipline in their lives and are willing to follow his commands. They are gentle toward their fellow humans. As it says in Titus 3:2, they "slander no one," they are "peaceable and considerate." They "show true humility toward all men." It is difficult to guess their position, stature, or wealth in life because they treat everyone as equals. On a hot day, they don't expect someone to get them water, they go and get water for everyone.

The meek are not easily angered. They are not provoked into foolish arguments or meaningless quarrels. They don't lose control and fly off in a fit of rage. They know how to respond to an insult with a kind word or a soft answer. When needed, they can still show their displeasure or disagreement toward a disturbing situation, but they themselves are not dragged into the indecency of it. They keep a level head when everyone else is losing theirs. To be meek is to be like God, who can become angry, but never loses control.

We are to learn from Jesus, who is "gentle and humble in heart."[1] The Bible says of him,

> *"A bruised reed he will not break, and a smoldering wick he will not snuff out, till he leads justice to victory." (Matthew 12:20)*

First and foremost, if we don't believe and understand that there will be a day of judgment, then we will find it difficult to grasp the idea of being meek. Jesus would not dismiss even a bruised reed or a smoldering wick. When the world is ready to cast aside something,

Jesus isn't. When we are weak in our faith, discouraged by life, drained of strength, Jesus doesn't kick us to the curb. He doesn't move on to someone else. He cares for us. He is patient with us. He knows our weaknesses and he is gentle with us. I once heard a brother say that God deals with us in the gentlest way possible to get us to listen to him.

Even when you feel like your faith is a smoldering wick that once was ablaze, but now has trouble staying lit, Jesus doesn't leave you. He doesn't forget you. Although the crowds may have moved on and the lights turned off, Jesus is still there for you. He knows you and cares for you. As it says in Matthew 21:5,

"'See, your king comes to you, gentle and riding on a donkey.'"

If we understand that there will be a day for the Lord to judge mankind, then we can imitate him by being gentle and humble in heart. We don't have to be the ones to dish out the discipline. We are the ones who dish out his love. We leave room for God to work. We are his humble servants, and even when we think we have surrendered ourselves completely to his word and power, and we think there isn't much more room for us to lower ourselves, we look down and see our King, our Master, our Lord—on his knees, washing not only our feet, but the feet of the one who would betray him.

Those who embrace Jesus' teaching would much rather forgive a hundred wrongs than retaliate for just one. We don't get even with others. We leave room for God to work, to bring someone to repentance. We know and understand that God cares for the other person too. The meek have possession of their own abilities and learn to control them, yet they also allow God to be in control. The meek learn how to rule their souls and control their spirits. They don't proclaim their own goodness, but praise the goodness of God. The meek can be put in any situation and not lose their footing. They are firm because they stand with God.

This is the one blessing that bestows a promise upon the here and now, for the meek "shall inherit the earth." Some have said that the earth in this verse represents the "new earth" of heaven, but I have come to understand that Jesus means *now*—that the meek will find a special place in this life, on this earth. The meek will be happy. Life opens up for people with meek characters. Good things happen when you don't lose your temper or go around promoting yourself and pumping yourself up with pride. You leave room for someone else to tell you that they appreciate you. They can still pat you on the back because your hand isn't there already patting yourself. People will want to work with you; they will enjoy being around you. Bosses won't fire you, even in difficult times. Others are happy to see you if you've been gone or out of town. Your presence is a welcome event, not something people dread. You are blessed because you enjoy life, your family and other people; you are fit for any relationship, situation or standing.

Although the world would portray the meek as being run-down and ridiculed, they are the ones with good health, good standing, and good associations. Each day comes easily. Worry doesn't weigh down their bones, and anxiety doesn't occupy their minds. They can be happy when they work and content when they rest. You would never know if they are living with worldly abundance or dwelling in poverty, because no matter what their circumstances, they are at peace with God.

I know that when I began to understand this teaching, life became much simpler for me. I had been putting too much pressure on myself to respond the way that the world thought I should respond. I had always felt the pressure to live up to the world's expectation for me. Instead, learning to be meek has made the burden of life so much lighter, because now I just concern myself with how God sees me.

When we truly embrace this teaching from Jesus, then life on this cue ball will begin to open up. I encourage you to spend time meditating on Jesus' teaching, figuring out how you can add to your faith the wisdom of being meek.

Stay Hungry

Blessed are those who hunger and thirst for righteousness, for they will be filled.

— Matthew 5:6

"Do you miss it?" My friend's expression was veiled, with a glint of desire sparking in his eyes.

I didn't need to ask what he meant. The thrill of the party life, the numbness of drugs, the false confidence of alcohol…My old life, the life I had surrendered to Jesus three years earlier, the life I had sworn to give up forever. The kind of wild life my Christian friend had also led, many years ago.

Did I miss it?

The answer was yes.

I'd spent the past three years enthusiastically throwing myself into the church and the service of Christ, setting my goals single-mindedly on becoming a preacher one day. My friend and I had become partners in the gospel, working together to save souls on college campuses. We were a formidable team for God. Ours was an easy and effective partnership—in part because we shared similar sinful backgrounds, and now the bond of a common love for Christ. I rarely gave a thought to my old ways, but now here they were, suddenly thrown back in my face again, catching me off-guard. And I was shocked to find the old desires stirring within me so quickly, awakening memories of my old life. Yes, I missed it. Yes, it had been fun. Yes...

Before I knew it, my friend and I had dragged one another back into the pit that Christ had helped us to escape—the secret life of drugs, alcohol, deceit. No one knew but the two of us—not our friends, not our families, not our wives.

And it all started with a desire that I thought I had crucified. A desire that turned into temptation, and led me so far from the narrow path I'd vowed to follow.

> *When tempted, no one should say, "God is tempting me." For God cannot be tempted by evil, nor does he tempt anyone; but each one is tempted when, by his own evil desire, he is dragged away and enticed. Then, after desire is conceived, it gives birth to sin; and sin, when it is full-grown, gives birth to death. (James 1:13-15)*

Desire is a powerful force, holding our future in its hands. I can't blame anyone for where I ended up at that time in my life. I was dragged away by my own evil desires.

The cravings within us drag us along through life. Sin starts at the level of our desire. If our inmost desires are for evil purposes, then we will arrive at a wicked end.

Sins only tempt us if they hit upon our desires. If we carry around unchecked lustful desires in our hearts, then we will be tempted by sexual sin. Someone who doesn't have a particular desire in their heart won't be tempted by the evil in front of them. They will dismiss it quickly and easily, but a person who has that desire within them will wrestle with the temptation. We all have our own set of evil desires, and we all must choose whether or not we will be honest with ourselves and with others about our particular temptations, and whether or not we will nurture them or nail them to the cross.

When I returned to my secret life of drugs and alcohol, I didn't know that I still desired my old way of life. I didn't know that the "yes" was still in my heart. I knew that I had repented of my sin when I got baptized, so I never gave it another thought, but I didn't know that the yearning was still in me—or maybe I just refused to admit it. I had never dealt with my sins at the desire level. I had never dealt with the cravings that lay deep in my heart, and the cravings took hold of me once more.

When desire and evil meet, they produce sin. I'll say that again. Really think about what it means: When desire and evil meet, they produce sin. If that sin is continually nurtured, caressed, and cuddled, it will finally produce death. At that point, there will be no hope for us.

It's not hard to take the next step into sin, if you have already been dragged to the precipice by your own desire. Since the desire to use drugs was still in my heart, it was an easy step for me to use drugs again when the opportunity arose. We are often shocked by what people do, but if we could see inside their heart, then we wouldn't be shocked, since their heart was already there to begin with. Their desire just needed to be presented with an opportunity for evil.

All of us must stop and examine our own desires. If it is love that you crave, then you will be dragged to where you believe you will find love. It's not God's fault if you believe you will find love at a nightclub or bar! If your desire is for money or power, then you will be dragged to where you can find them. We have to start by being honest with ourselves about what we truly want. What do you crave, what do you long for? What is it that you want to achieve in life, what are your goals? Once you get honest about what you want, then you have to see if it matches up with Jesus' commands, so that you can align your desires with righteousness.

Struggle Against Temptation

God has a way of exposing our inmost desires. If we cherish secret, sinful desires, they will one day come to the surface. As God told Cain when he wrestled with envy of his brother Abel,

> *"Sin is crouching at your door; it desires to have you, but you must master it." (Genesis 4:7)*

Even Jesus was tempted by Satan, and he used the scriptures to fend off Satan's attacks. And the Bible encourages us by saying,

For we do not have a high priest who is unable to sympathize with our weaknesses, but we have one who has been tempted in every way, just as we are—yet was without sin. Let us then approach the throne of grace with confidence, so that we may receive mercy and find grace to help us in our time of need. (Hebrews 4:15-16)

The good news is that God does not leave us unprepared for temptation. God knows our weaknesses, and provides for us even when we are tempted:

So, if you think you are standing firm, be careful that you don't fall! No temptation has seized you except what is common to man. And God is faithful; he will not let you be tempted beyond what you can bear. But when you are tempted, he will also provide a way out so that you can stand up under it. (1 Corinthians 10:12-13)

That fateful day when my friend suggested we return to our old sinful way of life, I had many ways out. I could have walked away; I could have confessed the temptation to my wife or to other spiritual friends; I could have turned to God in prayer. But I chose to walk away from God's ways out. I gave full sway to my sinful desires, and I reaped the consequences. Had I only dealt with my desires before they were in full bloom, how different the next several years of my life would have been! If we want to conquer sin, we must first conquer our desires.

Hunger and Thirst for Righteousness

But of course, not all desires are bad. Jesus tells us what we *should* seek: "Blessed are those who hunger and thirst for righteousness, for they will be filled." If we want to make it to the end, we must crave godliness above all else. We must hunger and thirst for righteousness every day. If righteousness had really been my greatest hunger all those years ago, then I would not have been dragged back into drug abuse.

We don't like feeling hungry—and yet it is one of our basic human needs. The unique thing about hunger is that it is satisfied only for a short while until it cries out to be made happy once again. Our appetites will always return as long as we are walking this earth. We can visit the most expensive restaurants and eat the finest foods, but they will only satisfy us for a short while. Our cravings, our hunger will eventually drive us back to the table for more, even within a few hours of eating our last meal.

The U.S. boasts a thriving multi-billion dollar industry whose goal is to help people to curb their appetite so they can lose weight. We all desire to gain control of our appetites. We all want to be the ruler of our stomachs, but sure enough, our hunger and thirst always return, and if unsatisfied long enough, they will eventually lead to death. Our bodies must be nourished with food and water. There is no way around that fact. How we choose to nourish our bodies is up to us, but we all require sustenance in some form every day.

The ever-surprising Jesus offers us another unexpected path toward happiness—through the unpleasant feeling of hunger. "Blessed are those who hunger and thirst for righteousness," he says. Hunger is uncomfortable, undesirable. We associate it with poverty. We prefer to live a life that is satisfied and filled.

But Jesus calls us to hunger and thirst—not for food, but for God. Righteousness begins with the inside. If you desire to do what is right in the eyes of God, then you will set your path in the direction of godliness and heaven.

Hunger and thirst go down to the very depths of our most basic human needs, down to our core, down into our souls. Our desire for righteousness must be our most basic pursuit. If we get up in the morning and head out the door, but find ourselves in the middle of the morning having spent no time with God, we should start to feel uncomfortable. Jesus calls us to make righteousness our most basic human need.

Jesus tells us that if we crave righteousness, we will be blessed, we will be filled. He alone will fill the emptiness in our soul and quench the thirst in our heart. Praise God for that promise!

But God's guarantee contains a spiritual paradox. Hungering and thirsting for righteousness is the only way we can experience true fulfillment, and yet we must *continue* to hunger and thirst for righteousness. We can be at peace and feel content, but in some ways, we are not meant to be completely satisfied in our spiritual journey. God never intended for us to be completely satisfied—not on this earth, anyway. Just as our physical appetites require consistent attention, so it is with our spiritual needs. We are not supposed to put our lives on cruise control—we must keep asking, keep seeking, keep knocking...keep hungering and thirsting for God.[1]

Make Every Effort

In Luke 13:24, when someone asks Jesus if only a few people will be saved, he replies,

> *"Make every effort to enter through the narrow door, because many, I tell you, will try to enter and will not be able to."*

The Greek word he uses is *agōnizomai*, which means to "to struggle, literally, to compete for a prize; apply ourselves with the utmost energy; agonize."[2] We are to agonize on this journey through life. We are not called to make a lazy attempt at our salvation. We must endure a great deal of pain as we go, taking earnest care with each step and with every decision. Making it to heaven will not just happen by accident or by osmosis. We won't arrive in eternal paradise because we were fortunate to catch a break. We must be diligent about our journey, taking great concern about our steps every day. We must be like Jacob, who "struggled with God and with men," and overcame.[3] We need to be like David, who wept and cried out to God for his deliverance.

We must continually strive in the direction of righteousness, always in pursuit of God's will and his desires. We must stay hungry and thirsty for God in the same way that physical hunger and thirst motivate us to work so that we can eat. Spiritually, we must search, seek, petition, and never let up. Our lives are at peace, but our desire is always for God. We can be content with what God has given us, but we strive to become more like him. We live knowing that we will never arrive at our destination, but we will always be in pursuit of it. We get in the car and set our GPS for righteousness.

Even in the midst of my drug abuse and deceit, when I was giving free rein to my evil desires, I came up empty—still hungry, still needy. Sinful desires promise us the world, but destroy our relationships; they offer us a high, but steal our joy; they entice us with freedom, but leave us enslaved.

Not so with righteousness. The consistent, wholehearted, humble pursuit of godliness is the only way to lasting peace, joy, and hope.

If it weren't for the grace of God extended to me through my amazing wife, who never gave up on me, and my friends, who supported me as I decided to change once and for all, I know that I would not be a Christian today—much less writing a book about following Jesus. My story reminds me that even when we fall—even when we believe the lie and embrace our sinful desires—God is faithful, and can bring us back. Even from the pit, we can hunger and thirst for God—and he hears our cry.

> *I waited patiently for the LORD;*
> *he turned to me and heard my cry.*
> *He lifted me out of the slimy pit,*
> *out of the mud and mire;*
> *he set my feet on a rock*
> *and gave me a firm place to stand.*
> *He put a new song in my mouth,*
> *a hymn of praise to our God.*
> *Many will see and fear*
> *and put their trust in the LORD.*
> *(Psalm 40:1-3)*

Share the Mercy

Blessed are the merciful, for they will be shown mercy.
— Matthew 5:7

We are a culture that doesn't offer much sympathy for mistakes. We are particularly fascinated when one of our favorite movie stars, sports heroes or politicians messes up. The bigger the star, the bigger the newsprint and the harsher the criticisms. When Tiger Woods was caught in his web of deceit and adultery, the entire nation could talk of nothing else. I found myself drawn in, pausing to listen as the newscasters dished out embarrassing updates, hour by hour. It reminds me of the way we slow down on a highway when we pass an accident. We find it compelling to pay attention to others' misery. We like to gasp in dismay and shake our heads at the disappointment. We have TV shows dedicated to uncovering the dirt on people's lives and then exposing it to the world. We call it "news," but my guess is that really, we like the gossip and slander because it makes us feel better about ourselves. Knowing that someone else is dealing with worse problems makes our own imperfect existence seem a little more bearable.

Now that we live in the age of technology, it's even harder to escape our past mistakes. You don't have to be a celebrity or a politician to be reminded of what you've done wrong—society has a way of keeping up with us. Whether it's a driving record, credit statement or police report, we can't run very far from the person we've been. We usually leave a nice long paper trail behind us, and if by chance we happen to forget, then someone can just hit "print," and our whole past comes back to life again. Just the other day, I was doing some banking on the phone, and they asked me a series of security questions. One question was, "At which address did you live in the past?" They listed a series of addresses, and the one I recognized was from almost twenty years ago. It sort of scared me to think what other information they are keeping filed away about me!

We find ourselves having to explain things all over again. We "coulda, shoulda, woulda..." Society isn't very forgiving of our past missteps, but society's long memory isn't our biggest problem; we can find ways to deal with bad driving records, credit statements, and even police reports. The real problem lies within our hearts. We carry around within ourselves the mistakes, regrets, and sins from our past. The moment we try to get going in a new, positive direction, we play the tape in our mind of our old blunders and remind ourselves of a list of reasons why we are no good, why we shouldn't be joyful, why we can't move forward in life. We pop our own balloon as soon as we inflate it. We carry around the pains of the past. We can't seem to shake them. They torment our thoughts and create an internal agony. Even as Christians who have been born again, some of us still carry around the past, unable to shake free from its grip. Regret, guilt, and shame can paralyze us in our tracks and prevent us from moving forward.

Let's take a look at the apostle Paul. He was a man converted to Christ, one of the most influential Christians of all time, instrumental in bringing the gospel message around the world. He started churches in many cities and brought many non-believers to Christ. When he paused for a moment to assess himself and compare himself to others, Paul said,

I have worked much harder, been in prison more frequently, been flogged more severely, and been exposed to death again and

again. Five times I received from the Jews the forty lashes minus one. Three times I was beaten with rods, once I was stoned, three times I was shipwrecked, I spent a night and a day in the open sea, I have been constantly on the move. I have been in danger from rivers, in danger from bandits, in danger from my own countrymen, in danger from Gentiles; in danger in the city, in danger in the country, in danger at sea; and in danger from false brothers. I have labored and toiled and have often gone without sleep; I have known hunger and thirst and have often gone without food; I have been cold and naked. Besides everything else, I face daily the pressure of my concern for all the churches. (2 Corinthians 11:23–28)

Paul tells us of all the suffering he has endured for Christ. He tells us of his labor. If you were to ask Paul about his service to the Lord, he wouldn't need to say a word. He could lift his shirt and show you the marks. If you were to total up all of the lashes that Paul received for Christ, they would add up to 195. Wounds opened up from Paul's body and blood flowed. He was physically persecuted so many times that the Bible doesn't record every incident in detail. We know the story of when Paul was nearly stoned to death, retold in Acts 14:19. After Paul was stoned, his enemies dragged his body outside the city, thinking Paul was dead. Picture that for a minute. His attackers, thinking they had gotten the job done, grabbed his arms and dragged his lifeless body through the dusty streets on their way to deposit him outside the city like garbage. His blood left a trail in the dirt. The crime scene was an easy one to figure out. CSI could have solved this one pretty fast. The red rocks told the story, and you could follow the trail of blood to the body, where Paul lay motionless. Shortly after that, the Bible says, in a typical understatement, "He got up and went back into the city." Wow!

I don't know about you, but my Christian résumé doesn't quite read like Paul's. In fact, there isn't much on his list of accomplishments that I could relate to—I've been hungry and tired at times, but that's about it. Paul's life for Christ is such that if we were both playing football, Paul would win the Heisman Trophy and I would be playing flag football. There is no comparison.

I am always amazed when I read 2 Corinthians 12:7, where Paul describes being given "a thorn in [his] flesh, a messenger of Satan, to torment [him]." The same Paul who suffered immensely for Christ was still burdened in his flesh with some weakness. Paul doesn't share with us exactly what his thorn was, but when he fasted and prayed for the Lord to remove the thorn, the Lord answered him by saying, "My grace is sufficient for you, for my power is made perfect in weakness."[1] Whatever the thorn was, Jesus told Paul that he would not remove it, because God's grace was enough. Even though Paul felt this tremendous burden in his flesh, the Lord allowed it to continue, because Paul had grace to cover it.

If that is how life was for the apostle Paul, then what about us? What about the burdens we feel? Should we expect every burden to be lifted so we will feel better? Is that what Christianity is about, or are we supposed to learn that God's grace is sufficient for us? If the thorn had been removed from Paul's flesh, then how would he have ever learned about God's mercy? If the apostle Paul wasn't allowed to be burden-free in his walk with Jesus, but was told to rely on the grace that was given him, then how much more should you and I do the same thing? Just like with Paul, God wants his grace to shine brighter in our lives through our weaknesses and struggles. How much more do we need to know the grace of God in our lives? How much more is God trying to get us to lean on his grace and not on our own efforts?

The pagan religions of the past tried to appease their gods with ceremonies and rituals. The worshipers did things that they thought would earn the goodwill of their false gods. Our God, the God of heaven and earth, has never been like that. He doesn't need to be appeased. He already is the God of love, the God of mercy, no matter what we do. His love is already confirmed. It doesn't grow based on our performance. His love just is.

That doesn't mean we get a free pass to live as we please. When we sin, amends must be made. Because of God's great holiness, we could never enter his presence if his love and mercy had not already provided the sacrifice necessary to make us clean. Without cleansing from Jesus' blood, we would be exposed to God's wrath. Jesus' sacrifice comes from God's mercy and allows us to be right with God, but God's love doesn't change based on what we do.

In light of all this, who are we to be in this life? Jesus tells us, "Blessed are the merciful, for they will be shown mercy." The Greek word for *mercy* is *elehaymon*, "the act of feeling sympathy for the misery of another, but especially sympathy manifested in action."[2] Jesus calls us to share mercy with others in this life. He wants us to go out and empathize with others, to understand what they are going through. If Christians still carry around some measure of guilt and burden from their past sins, even though they know the truth and have been completely cleansed, how much more do the children of the world carry the burden of unforgiven sin? We are to listen and understand, but we are also to act. We are to introduce people to God's love, forgiveness, and mercy. We are to share with others the forgiveness that we ourselves have received. The world needs to know! The world needs to hear! We don't just sympathize to make people feel better, but after we listen to them, we help them to initiate a relationship with God. We help them to know God their Father. We are servants of God, instruments that he uses to reach a lost world.

It is much easier to tell ourselves that the world isn't interested in knowing God than to deny ourselves and go out searching for the noble few who are seeking God. This truth stands in contrast to the attitude taken by the Pharisees and Sadducees of Jesus' day. They were strict and rigid with the world, passing judgment on everyone they saw. They were too proud and conceited to extend God's mercy to the world; it was much easier to condemn everyone but themselves. As instruments for God, we should not bind up his mercy, but share it with the world.

Contrary to what the world thinks, Christians are not here to judge others living with them on this cue ball; one speck is not meant to criticize another speck. Jesus tells us how we are to deal with the faults of others. He tells us not to judge, but to share God's mercy, share the good news. We are to extend mercy both to the world and to our brothers and sisters in Christ. We are not supposed to hoard it or keep it for ourselves. God's mercy is to be shared abundantly.

The amazing thing is that when we deny ourselves—deny our feelings, our emotions, our tiredness—and go out and help the world to know God, Jesus tells us that we will be the happy ones. We will be blessed. When we teach the world about the love of God, we will experience true joy, internal happiness. Although we go out to bless, we ourselves are blessed.

Live Purely

Blessed are the pure in heart, for they will see God.
— Matthew 5:8

It is here in the sixth beatitude that we find the most inspiring and condemning of all Christ's statements. Jesus says, "Blessed are the pure in heart, for they will see God." Anyone who truly desires to have a relationship with God can be inspired and encouraged by the statement that the pure in heart will be able to see God. The pure in heart will have their faith confirmed by seeing the God that they worship. When our hearts are pure in our relationship with God, then we will see him and know him. We will be inspired by his presence in our lives and encouraged by his company as we walk each day. This is what we desire: to see God. We want to see his glory and be awed by his love, inspired by his power, humbled by his mercy. We want to see this every day of our lives.

The pure will see God, but what about the impure? They will not see God. People who live in the impurity of this world, who allow iniquity to rule their hearts and reign in their bodies, will never know God or even come close to seeing God. They are condemned by their impure hearts and by the filth in their lives.

When we allow sin to dwell in our hearts, when we let our evil desires stay unchanged, then we will be blocked from seeing God. Our religion will become empty and hollow. Our religion will become one rule to the next rule. Christian life will become a miserable existence, and we will be weighed down by the burden. I can remember a brother I once knew in the fellowship, a strong Christian who was married and had a couple of children. But in a short period of time, he began coming to church less and less, then finally stopped coming to church altogether. He had joined a band with some friends and decided that Christianity was too much of a burden for him, so he left. Several months later, he returned. When I asked him why he came back, he said, "I have had the burden of Christianity, and I have had the burden of the world. I much prefer the burden of Christianity."

When we let sin creep into our hearts, it prevents us from seeing God work in our lives. When we can't see God working in our lives, then Christianity becomes a burden. Imagine there is a painting on the wall in front of you, and you are asked to describe it. What does it look like? What colors are prominent? Describe the scene. Now imagine standing before that same painting, but with someone holding a hand in front of your eyes. Could you describe the painting? Absolutely not! Not only would you be unable to describe the painting, but you could not even confirm its existence. Sin has the same effect upon our relationship with God.

Hebrews 3:12 says, "See to it, brothers, that none of you has a sinful, unbelieving heart that turns away from the living God." Sin hardens our hearts and blocks us from seeing God. When we have sin in our hearts, we can no longer see God working in our lives and we find it easy to walk away from God. Sin pollutes our hearts and keeps out the life-giving glory of God. We have to first deal with the sin in our lives, and then everything else will become clear. Jesus came and first called everyone to "repent, for the kingdom of God is near."[1] The kingdom of God is always near in our lives; we only have to get rid of the filth that clouds our relationship with God.

Jesus gives one of his strongest rebukes to the Pharisees and teachers of the law when he says,

"Woe to you, teachers of the law and Pharisees, you hypocrites! You clean the outside of the cup and dish, but inside they are full of greed and self-indulgence. Blind Pharisee! First clean the inside of the cup and dish, and then the outside also will be clean.

"Woe to you, teachers of the law and Pharisees, you hypocrites! You are like whitewashed tombs, which look beautiful on the outside but on the inside are full of dead men's bones and everything unclean. In the same way, on the outside you appear to people as righteous but on the inside you are full of hypocrisy and wickedness." (Matthew 23:25–28)

The word *hypocrite*, the Greek word *hupokrites*, is used in Matthew fifteen times by Jesus. He uses the word to describe the teachers of the law and the Pharisees. The meaning of the word is "an actor under an assumed character, a stage player."[2] Jesus says that the religious leaders are no different than actors in a play. They look the part, but behind the mask we find a totally different person. They are not who they appear to be. To be a hypocrite is to be in a terrible place. Your religion becomes meaningless. It's not bad enough that hypocrites are headed for destruction, but they destroy others along the way. As Jesus says in Matthew 23:13–15,

"Woe to you, teachers of the law and Pharisees, you hypocrites! You shut the kingdom of heaven in men's faces. You yourselves do not enter, nor will you let those enter who are trying to... You travel over land and sea to win a single convert, and when he becomes one, you make him twice as much a son of hell as you are."

The Pharisees were supposed to be the ones to teach the way of Moses and the prophets. They were the ones who should have spotted the Messiah first, but instead they taught against Jesus and poisoned people's minds against him. They were blind guides. They confused Jesus' doctrine and ignored his miracles. They used all their strength and knowledge against the kingdom of God instead of for it. They wore their religion on the outside, but their insides were full of lust, greed, malice, hatred, deceit, envy, jealousy, and bitterness. They looked the part, but inside they were far from it.

Jesus tells them that they should have worked on their hearts first. They should have cleaned the inside of the cup instead of the outside. It's fitting that Jesus would use the simple illustration of a cup to illustrate his point. There is no way to get anything clean out of a dirty cup. You might manage to get something clean off of a dirty plate, but a cup contains liquid that will mix with everything inside of it. You cannot get away with a dirty cup; it pollutes all of its contents. It will spoil whatever is put inside.

I once demonstrated this concept when teaching a children's class. I held up two cups—one was clean on the outside but dirty on the inside, the other was clean on the inside but dirty on the outside. I held the cups up so the kids could not see the insides, just the outside. I asked them, "Which cup would you like to drink from?" They all quickly and emphatically pointed to the one that looked clean on the outside. I told them, "Okay." I then showed them the inside of the cups. They all gasped and screamed in horror, because I had put bugs, dirt, and worms on the inside of the clean-looking cup. I then began to pour water into the cup and told them that they were going to have to drink from it. They all began to edge away from me as if they were going to run out of the room. After I let them off the hook, we sat and discussed the difference between outward appearances and what is really inside. They got the point: The inside matters most.

God is more concerned with our insides—our thoughts, our feelings, our character. He wants to rule the dominion of our hearts. He wants to be Lord of our insides, not just the outside. God wants *all* of our hearts; he wants our total devotion, from the inside out. One mistake that parents often make is that they only discipline the *actions* of their children. They correct behavior, but they fail to find out what is going on inside the child's heart, and so they do not teach their child how to have the right attitude.

We have to deal with the filth that is contained within us. God knows it's there. He doesn't just know it's there; he even sees the motives we hold deep down inside.

"And you, my son Solomon, acknowledge the God of your father, and serve him with wholehearted devotion and with a willing mind, for the LORD searches every heart and understands every motive behind the thoughts. If you seek him, he will be found by you; but if you forsake him, he will reject you forever."
(1 Chronicles 28:9)

We may not even realize the evil desires that exist within our hearts, but the filth can't be allowed to stay in our hearts, causing our insides to rot.

What is hidden in your heart? What do you hold deep down inside that, if it were exposed to others, would cause them to gasp, scream, and run for the door? What is preventing you from seeing God in your life, blocking you from seeing his splendor? What is covering the eyes of your heart so that you are unable see the glory of God?

It is almost impossible to clean the inside of a cup and not have the outside affected. The outside usually takes care of itself. If we deal with the stuff that hides deep down in our hearts, the sins that go against God's plan for our lives, the outside will take care of itself— our actions and appearance will follow our hearts. We are going to want to go to church. We will look forward to spending time with God. Our prayer times will increase and intensify. We will love our neighbors easily and naturally. Doing good will become second nature. Sharing our faith will be a passion we cannot suppress. When we see our brothers, we won't hide, but we will embrace them and encourage them. We will give to those in need with a joyful spirit. The burden of our Christianity will be light.

Begin by denying sin a foothold in your life. Start by saying "no" to the sin that lives within you. What sin is crouching at your door?[3] What sin grips you the moment you walk out the door in the morning, or grabs hold of your heart when no one else is around? Jesus tells us that we don't have to worry about dealing with sin the rest of our lives—we just have to deal with it today! Focus on getting the sin out of your life today. You have the strength to make the decision right now. The next time you are tempted, turn away, turn it off, deny the thoughts, and ignore the devil. You will grow in strength against the evil forces. God has equipped you with everything you need to fight this battle, but you have to fight. You can't just surrender to the enemy. You cannot admit defeat. You are a warrior for Christ. As Ephesians 6:12 says, "...our struggle is not against flesh and blood..." The battle is within you. The battle is for your heart. Jesus gave us the victory on the cross, and you are on his side. Don't surrender to the enemy. Jesus bought your heart with his blood. You cannot just hand yourself back to the enemy.

If sin has a foothold in your life, if you have become powerless in its grip, then sit down with another Christian to talk about it. Ask for their prayers. Once you clean the inside of the cup, you will be free to fill your cup with good things. The battle is only half-won when you rid your heart of evil—we have more work to do! We have to make sure our cup doesn't just get cleaned and then remain empty. In a related analogy, Jesus tells us,

> *"When an evil spirit comes out of a man, it goes through arid places seeking rest and does not find it. Then it says, 'I will return to the house I left.' When it arrives, it finds the house unoccupied, swept clean and put in order. Then it goes and takes with it seven other spirits more wicked than itself, and they go in and live there. And the final condition of that man is worse than the first. That is how it will be with this wicked generation." (Matthew 12:43–45)*

We must allow God to fill our cup, our house, with his Spirit, his love, and his mission, because as we will see in the next verse, the subject of our next chapter, "Blessed are the peacemakers..."

Spread the Peace

Blessed are the peacemakers, for they will be called sons of God.

— Matthew 5:9

We've all been there before: The week has been crazy, work is hectic, the kids are especially rowdy, the phone doesn't stop ringing; we have emails, voicemails, and faxes. When we try to cross one item off our to-do list, two more get added. We get out of bed and jump right onto the treadmill of life. We know that we can't stop running or else we'll be thrown off. We tell ourselves to keep running, to keep up the pace, it will slow down soon. We tell our friends, "Let's get together," but we know there isn't a chance of it actually happening. We're too busy, too exhausted. We don't have the time. Life is out of control. We feel like someone has installed a bowling alley in our home. The noise, the chaos, the busyness, the running around—we can't find even a few minutes to catch our breath or collect our thoughts.

Then our mind drifts. It drifts to the vacation we have planned, or just the fantasy of a vacation. We daydream about our time off, our time for peace.

We all long for a break from the chaos, for rest from the busy lives we live. We go from work, to soccer, to homework, to baths, to more homework, bills, phone calls, and then finally to bed. We want to be able to kick back and relax without the craziness of life coming in and stealing the moment. We think it can be found on a beach on some distant island, or at a luxurious spa in some isolated part of the world. We believe the peace we crave is just beyond our reach, or just out of our price range.

Jesus tells us that peace can be found right where we sit—in the middle of the craziness and chaos. Peace is not hiding on some beach somewhere, or tucked away in the mountains of Nepal. Peace is found in the kingdom of God. The reason we can't find peace in this world is because we are not at peace with God. Jesus rebukes the Pharisees when he tells them, "If you, even you, had only known on this day what would bring you peace—but now it is hidden from your eyes."[1]

They didn't know what would bring them peace.

We can find peace with God in his kingdom. Consider the parable Jesus tells about the two kings about to go to war:

"Or suppose a king is about to go to war against another king. Will he not first sit down and consider whether he is able with ten thousand men to oppose the one coming against him with twenty thousand? If he is not able, he will send a delegation while the other is still a long way off and will ask for terms of peace. In the same way, any of you who does not give up everything he has cannot be my disciple." (Luke 14:31–33)

First, consider the two kings. The first king, having only ten thousand men, has the smaller army, less strength, fewer resources; he is no match for the second king and his twenty thousand soldiers. The first king is going to lose the war. He does not stand a chance. It would be foolishness for him to try and do battle.

In this parable, you and I are represented by the smaller king with the smaller army. We are the ones who, at the end of our lives, will face God—the larger king with the larger army. God is coming to judge the world. God is coming to make war against our kingdom. He is coming to destroy those who have set themselves up against him.

In a sense, we all think of ourselves as "kings" in this world. We have our own little kingdoms. We go where we want, think what we want, say what we want, watch what we want, and we are subject to no one. We are the kings of our own domain. We may think of ourselves as kings even if we are not successful or powerful in the eyes of the world. We may not have money, power, or prestige, but we still live by our own rules. We set the laws for our ourselves and we decide when we will act and whom we will follow. Granted, some kingdoms may be better in certain respects than others; some may be more wealthy or powerful than others, but we all think of ourselves as masters of our own domains.

Jesus came to tell us that this isn't acceptable. God is coming, and he's going to make war against the kingdoms of the earth. He's coming with fire. He's coming for the Day of Judgment. Jesus tells us that if we are wise, "while the king is still a long way off," we will sit down with him and make peace. We will find out the conditions of surrender. What are the terms for laying down our arms? We have to make peace with the bigger, stronger king; otherwise, we will be destroyed when he comes. We can't think, "Because I am a 'good' king compared to others, God will let me go." We are destined to lose the battle, so we must find out what the winning king requires.

Once we surrender our kingdom to the larger king, then we become a subject in his kingdom—we are no longer kings. We give up our crown and our territory, and take up citizenship in his kingdom. God himself becomes our king, and we are subject to his authority, his rules, and his word. The king can come in and take whatever he wants because we are now just subjects in his kingdom. We surrender all.

God's kingdom is no longer defined by borders or boundaries as it was in the Old Testament. God doesn't rule over an allotted territory or region. He doesn't rule our land; he rules our hearts. God is the king of hearts. The borders and boundaries are within us, and we surrender to his rule from the inside, not the outside.

Those of us who belong to God have peace in our hearts. We have abdicated our throne, and God now sits in his rightful place, as ruler of our hearts. We no longer live, because he lives in us, and we are a part of his kingdom.[2] We no longer bear the burden of controlling our own kingdom—we have entrusted that responsibility to someone much wiser and more capable than we are!

We find peace when we allow God to reign inside of us. I have traveled to some of the most luxurious beaches in the world, resting as far away from the day–to–day busyness as I could get, but if I wasn't at peace with God, I still did not find peace, even in so-called "paradise."

When we make our thoughts, opinions, and feelings subject to God's commands, we find peace in this world. When we submit our desires to his word, then we can rest. The world may fall apart around us, but we have peace because God lives within us. In the midst of a storm, Jesus slept on a cushion in the stern of a boat. Everyone else was panicking, but Jesus was resting.[3] When his disciples woke him up, Jesus challenged their faith!

Once we make our own peace with God, Jesus tells us that happiness comes from becoming peacemakers. And not only do we find joy, we also become true sons of God! We are meant not just to keep the peace and joy we find in our Father's kingdom for ourselves. We are called to go out and share it with others. We are meant to teach others about God's kingdom and usher them into the peace that we ourselves enjoy. We can't accomplish such a task by just being a good person. We must actively teach others to accept God's "terms of peace." This kind of transformation is a battle, as most people enjoy being the ruler of their own lives and resist becoming subject to another king. Those who are wise will surrender to God's conditions.

The mind of sinful man is death, but the mind controlled by the Spirit is life and peace; the sinful mind is hostile to God. It does not submit to God's law, nor can it do so. Those controlled by the sinful nature cannot please God. (Romans 8:6–8)

The world is hostile towards God. It does not want to submit to God's word or authority. Salvation is not achieved based on how "nice" someone is, or how many good deeds they do. It comes through surrendering our will to God. At the end of our lives, many of us think that God is going to take out a list of all the good things we've done and a list of all the bad things we've done, and if the list of good is longer than the list of bad, then we are okay; but if the list of bad is longer than the list of good, then we go to hell. That's not how it's going to work! The test will be whether we accepted the terms of peace that God spelled out for us in the Bible.

Since the world is so confused, those of us who know God and understand what it takes to follow him must spread the truth! We must go out and make disciples of Jesus. We must go out and help others to surrender to God's authority. And what joy we can bring to the world! As God's ambassadors of peace, we introduce a lost, burdened, and weary world to real peace—peace that will last. We show people where to find the rest they long for, the internal peace that is not found on a beach or faraway mountain.

Peace can be found right where we sit. It starts between us and God, because his eternal peace starts with our internal surrender.

Follow Righteously

Blessed are those who are persecuted because of righteousness,
for theirs is the kingdom of heaven.

—Matthew 5:10

The four of them were most likely friends as they grew up. They probably lived anywhere from two to five miles apart. If this was a modern-day story, then they probably would have competed against each other in sports, possibly attended rival high schools or even the same high school. They would have hung out in the same places and known the same friends. Perhaps they were the best of friends. Their families would have known one another, since they were in the same line of work together, and since they had boys the same age, you could imagine a strong family friendship developing. But this story happened two thousand years ago, so the four boys most likely didn't compete against each other in sports; instead, they probably developed a friendship through the family businesses, fishing. They would have purchased their materials from the same suppliers and sold their goods in the same markets. They all fished in the same waters, and as is a custom with fishermen, they helped one another. Fishing is one of those rare industries where rivalry takes a back seat to camaraderie; one fisherman helping another fisherman is just an unspoken rule.

Yes, you can envision the two brothers, Simon and Andrew, spending time with the other pair of brothers, James and John. They probably did what boys do: They wrestled, threw stones, fooled around on their fathers' boats, and just hung out while the adults worked. As they grew, their characters formed, as did their relationships with one another. It's not surprising that later on in life they would be so comfortable with one another that they could argue about who was the greatest. They probably had the very same argument as kids!

Later, Simon and Andrew moved their business to Capernaum, where James and John also lived. This was better for the trade, a bigger city with more opportunity.

We also know that the four had more in common than just fishing. They went out to see John the Baptist. James and John were Zealots, which meant that they despised the Roman establishment. They must have all had expectations for the coming of the Jewish Messiah. They had hoped the Messiah would come and overthrow the government, that he would lead them to victory the way King David had done. He would unify Israel and establish the Jews as the dominant race. James and John, named the "Sons of Thunder" by Jesus, were ready to fight. They would do whatever it took to establish Israel. They put their hope in God to deliver them from the oppression of the Roman regime. They only needed someone to say the word and they would die for the cause. It's possible and not unlikely that the four bonded their relationship through these convictions.

So when the four of them went to see John the Baptist, they may have been ready for some good old-fashioned, hard-core teaching. Could John possibly be the one to lead the revolution? They had heard about this guy, but they wanted to see and hear for themselves. Andrew was one of the first to follow John the Baptist. He heard John point to Jesus and say, "Look, the Lamb of God!", and then Andrew began following Jesus.[1] Right away, Andrew went to find his brother Simon to take him to Jesus. Andrew uttered the five words to his brother that would change history forever: "We have found the Messiah."[2]

Andrew brought his brother to Jesus, and Jesus looked at Simon and knew him already. The first thing Jesus did was set a goal for Simon: "You will be called Cephas." Another way to say it would be, "Today you are known as Simon, but you will be the rock." Peter would become a crucial part of the foundation of the church to come. This fisherman, who would be known as much for his mistakes as he was known for his victories, would become the rock for the church. Jesus saw him and knew him right away. This was Peter, the first to speak and often the first to be wrong. He had the unfortunate distinction of being the only disciple whom Jesus himself would call "Satan."[3]

The four friends would continue to be wrong as they followed Jesus. Jesus wouldn't tell them to strap on a sword; he showed them how be meek. He wouldn't teach them to hate the government; he taught them how to be merciful. He wouldn't teach them to be the kind of leaders they thought they should be; he taught them to be great by washing their feet.

Jesus would take these fiery few and turn them into pillars of the church. He took John the Zealot and turned him into the "apostle of love." They would be transformed from men who were ready to take a life, to men giving life. If this were a script written by man, then it would most likely depict the Messiah taking the apostle of love and turning him into the Son of Thunder, but this story wasn't written by man. These men were transformed by the hand of God. They had found the Messiah. What started out as just a walk with a man who they thought might be just another rabbi, became a walk with God. These four would become the key component of Jesus' plan for changing the world, but they weren't ready for him, and neither was the world.

One of the most powerful interactions between Jesus and his disciples occurs when Jesus tells Peter,

"Simon, Simon, Satan has asked to sift you as wheat. But I have prayed for you, Simon, that your faith may not fail. And

when you have turned back, strengthen your brothers." (Luke 22:31-32)

The picture Jesus paints is intense. Somewhere in the heavenly realms, Satan had asked God for permission to sift Peter, test Peter, and break him down: "Hey God, let's find out if this guy Peter is for real." Sure anyone can be devoted when they see the miracles and receive the encouragement and love of Christ every day, but what happens when we're really tested, when we're challenged to the core? When Peter is squeezed, what will come out? Will the fruit of God emerge, or the ugly stuff—the fear, doubt, and worry? This is Peter the fisherman—rugged, tough, a guy who was not afraid to mix it up. Peter thought he was "ready to go with [Jesus] to prison and to death."[4] And God allowed Satan to test him, to crush him down to his core.

A little girl recognized Peter while he was awaiting Jesus' trial in the courtyard, and called him out. Reacting on impulse and instinct, Peter lied...just as many of us would do. We like to think that we would react differently, with greater courage, but when pressed to the point of life and death, would we risk our lives to stand by Jesus? I believe this is the work that God is refining in us all our Christian lives, a faith in God so strong that we would be willing to die for him.

Peter lied three times when he was confronted that night. He emphatically cursed, to make his point. Peter was standing so close to Jesus when he said these things that Jesus turned and looked at him—and it was then that Peter remembered what Jesus had told him at their last supper together: "I tell you, Peter, before the rooster crows today, you will deny three times that you know me."[5]

Peter's first impulse and response was to deny Jesus. The Gospels tell us that Peter then went out and wept bitterly. His weeping was understandable—after all, he thought that his denial was the last thing Jesus would ever hear him say. For three days, Peter mourned the brutal crucifixion of his friend, knowing that the last words Jesus heard him speak had been a heartbreaking betrayal. In Peter's mind, that was it. Death was final. You don't come back from that.

It's no surprise that within a few days, Peter returned to fishing. "I'm going out to fish," Peter told his friends.[6] He was probably going to drive himself crazy if he sat around thinking about Jesus' death. That's the reality of death, he thought—you have to push on with life, you have to find a way to move forward. Peter went back to what he knew: fishing. But it's also no surprise that when Peter saw the resurrected Jesus walking on the beach, he jumped out of the boat to go to him. He had to see for himself and he couldn't wait for the boat, the boat was just going to take too long to get there. What a sight that must have been: Peter plowing through the water, swimming to the shore. Then, dripping wet, he stood before Jesus once again.

At this point, I don't imagine Peter was so quick with his words. He had nothing to boast about, no great claim, nothing to profess. He had been crushed. He had denied his friend and his Lord. What can you say after that? How do you begin to explain yourself? His failure might not have seemed so devastating had he not been such a braggadocio the night before his public denial, boasting at the Last Supper that he was prepared to die with Jesus. Now here he stood before Jesus, sopping wet and speechless.

What was it that needed to be sifted from Peter's character, from his heart? What was so important for him to change that the Lord was willing to let his friend go through this pain? We know that Jesus wanted Peter to feed his sheep.[7] Jesus wanted Peter to feed his sheep when he came back from Satan's test. Could it be that if Peter was going to go on and become a great teacher for Christ, to lead thousands upon thousands into the kingdom of heaven, that Peter needed to understand mercy and compassion a little bit more? Was it possible that Peter still didn't understand this concept? It's not hard to see that Peter was going to teach many people, but had he not been sifted, perhaps he would have been a bit self-righteous, arrogant and impatient toward the other sheep. After all, he had spent three years with Jesus, and he was the one hand-picked to lead. He was the man of the hour, the keeper of the keys of the kingdom,[8] and it's possible that he might not have shown mercy to others who followed Christ imperfectly. Before Peter's denial, maybe he just didn't understand or tolerate the weakness of others. Perhaps he had lacked compassion when others fell short; but now that he had been humbled, now that he himself had done the unthinkable, and Jesus had restored him through mercy and love, *now* Peter understood grace.

I think the most amazing part of this story is that God allowed Peter to go through all of this in order to make him into the leader that God wanted him to be. Peter had a ways to go in his character, but Jesus was already there.

So now, after all they had learned from their teacher, it was fitting that just a short time later, Peter ended up back in Jerusalem alongside his old friend John. One afternoon, the two friends walked together to the temple to pray.[9] They had learned righteousness from Jesus, and now they were living it.

A crippled man asked them for some money. Peter and John didn't have any money, but they gave the crippled man what they had. They healed him, saying, "In the name of Jesus Christ of Nazareth, walk." They wanted to make it clear exactly what they were giving the man: not money, but a new life in the name of Jesus. Many people came running to see what happened, so Peter and John just started telling the story of Jesus.

The two of them were simply doing what was right. They weren't trying to provoke anyone, they weren't trying to start a fight.

They simply started to witness for Jesus by telling the story. They'd had a front- row seat to the greatest event ever on the face of earth and now they were just re-telling the story. They had learned to obey, they had become like Jesus themselves, and now they were telling the story.

A funny thing happened—something they didn't expect, even though Jesus had warned them that it would happen. Their preaching disturbed the priests and the Sadducees. They disrupted the order of things, and so they were thrown in jail. When they were brought out before the high priests, they were questioned, and in their answer they had no choice but to tell the story again.[10] They weren't teaching a lesson; they hadn't prepared a sermon for the moment. They had no cool illustrations or great new insights; they simply started to tell the story of Jesus.

Peter and John went out from there and prayed with their brothers Andrew and James, and with the rest of the disciples. They prayed that they could speak with great boldness. That they would not be afraid and that they could continue to tell the story in the face of the threats.[11] After that prayer, the four brothers, along with the rest of the apostles, went out and performed great miracles, and many people came to believe.

As more and more people came to believe in Jesus, the high priest and Sadducees were filled with jealousy. They arrested the apostles and put them in jail, but an angel came and opened their cells and told them to go out into the temple courts, and "tell the people the full message of this new life."[12] They went out from the jail and began to preach.

Soon they found themselves in front of the high priest and Sadducees again. So Peter, John and the other apostles started to tell Jesus' story again, claiming, "We must obey God rather than men!"[13] The religious leaders became furious, so after some debate they had the apostles flogged and ordered them not to speak in the name of Jesus again. Acts 5:41 tells us, "The apostles left the Sanhedrin, rejoicing because they had been counted worthy of suffering disgrace for the Name."

The paradox continues. They celebrated because they were flogged. They rejoiced because they were persecuted. Why were they so happy? How can someone be happy after being flogged? You would be hard-pressed to find another prisoner in jail rejoicing after they had been flogged, but the apostles remembered that Jesus had told them at the beginning, "Blessed are those who are persecuted because of righteousness, for theirs is the kingdom of heaven."

What was it that made them happy? What taught these fishermen to rejoice after they had been persecuted? The answer is that they had finally become like Jesus. They were doing what Jesus had done and teaching what he had taught, and now they were being treated like he was treated. What an honor!

Persecution is the greatest compliment to our faith. It's the greatest tribute to a Christian life. When we go on living the life we are called to live, obeying the word of God and teaching others to do the same, if we receive persecution, it means we are like Jesus, our teacher and Lord.

When Jesus appeared to the apostles on the beach after his resurrection, he prepared breakfast for them, and as they sat there eating, Jesus asked Peter three times, "Do you love me?"[14] Jesus then told Peter that he would one day die for his faith. One day Peter would be put to death for what he was going to do and preach. Jesus concluded by telling Peter, "Follow me!" A lot had happened since the first time Jesus called Peter to follow him three years earlier; now Jesus was calling him to follow him to death. Jesus had shown him the way. He had walked the path ahead of Peter, and now it was Peter's turn.

And so, several weeks later, when Jesus' words began to come true, and Peter and the others began to receive persecution, they rejoiced because they had been chosen to receive the beautiful message of life. They rejoiced that not only had they heard the message, but now they were becoming like their teacher—this was a cause for celebration, even though the world would never understand it.

When we live the life Jesus has called us to live, and accept the teachings he has given us to teach, when we recognize that we are a speck on the face of this giant cue ball, called to have faith in the almighty God, we will be persecuted.

This is something to celebrate and rejoice about, just as Peter and his friends did, because "…great is [our] reward in heaven."[15] Amen!

Peter, Andrew, James and John—four lifelong friends—were shaped by the Master. Jesus was the potter and they were the clay. They had so much to change and such a long way to go. They were torn down and built back up. Who could have ever imagined that the legacy of friendships that began in a small fishing village would still be talked about two thousand years later? Four boys, who once played on boats while learning to fish, became courageous men whose convictions changed the world. Together they met Jesus;

together they watched him die and saw him rise again; together they became bold men of God who were counted worthy of suffering for the name of Jesus. Let us follow in their footsteps, banding together with our fellow Christians to live as Jesus did, to preach his message, and to rejoice when we too are counted worthy of suffering for his name.

Notes

Chapter 1 – The Cue Ball

1. *7 Natural Wonders,* http://sevennaturalwonders.org/
   north-america/yosemite-national-park (2008).

Chapter 2 – A Moment in Time

1. Joel E. Cohen, "Demographic Research: Life expectancy
   is the death-weighted average of the reciprocal of the
   survival-specific force of mortality," *Demographic
   Research* 22, no. 5 (January 22, 2010), http://www.
   demographic-research.org/Volumes/Vol22/5/22-5.pdf.
2. Khushnuma Irani, "Mosquito Life Cycle," Buzzle.com,
   http://www.buzzle.com/articles/mosquito-life-cycle.
   html (accessed July 8, 2010).
3. James 4:14
4. Genesis 8:1

Chapter 3 – A Wise Beginning

1. Proverbs 9:10
2. Proverbs 10:1

Chapter 4 – The Humble Creation

1. 1 Peter 1:7

Chapter 5 – Faith, Not Religion

1. Matthew 17:20; Luke 17:6
2. Mark 10:45

Chapter 6 – Directing Our Faith

1. 1 Corinthians 11:1

2. 1 Thessalonians 5:12-13, Hebrews 13:7,17
3. 1 Corinthians 13:7

Chapter 8 – Finishing the Faith Verse

1. *Webster's New World Dictionary of the American Language: 2nd College Edition* (The World Publishing Company, 1970)
2. Ibid.

Chapter 10 – Men of Certainty

1. 1 Samuel 17:23
2. 1 Samuel 17:26; 36

Chapter 11 – Cue Ball Victory

1. Revelation 5:10
2. Job 17:11

Chapter 12 – Faith, Not Time

1. Exodus 3:13-14
2. Revelation 21:6
3. 2 Corinthians 13:8

Chapter 13 – A Sure Man

1. 1 Kings 16:30
2. Jeremiah 19:5
3. 1 Kings 17:1
4. 1 Kings 18:19
5. 1 Kings 18:21
6. Matthew 21:22
7. James 5:17

Chapter 14 – The Certain Three

1. Proverbs 16:9

Chapter 15 – The Goal of Grace

1. 2 Samuel 11:1–27
2. 1 Samuel 13:14

Chapter 16 – Pursue Poverty

1. Luke 18:24
2. Colossians 2:3
3. 1 Corinthians 15:9
4. Ephesians 3:8

Chapter 17 – Mourn Continually

1. 1 Samuel 18:7
2. Jeremiah 9:1
3. Jeremiah 6:15
4. Jeremiah 6:14
5. Charles Caldwell Ryrie, *Ryrie Study Bible Expanded Edition* (Chicago: Moody Press, 1983), 1233.

Chapter 18 – Tread Lightly

1. Matthew 11:29

Chapter 19 – Stay Hungry

1. Matthew 7:7-8
2. Rick Meyers, *E-Sword: Version 9.5.1, Strong's Hebrew and Greek Dictionaries,* G75.
3. Genesis 32:28

Chapter 20 – Share the Mercy

1. 2 Corinthians 12:9
2. Rick Meyers, *E-Sword: Version 9.5.1, Strong's Hebrew and Greek Dictionaries*, G1655.

Chapter 21 – Live Purely

1. Matthew 3:2
2. Rick Meyers, *E-Sword: Version 9.5.1, Strong's Hebrew and Greek Dictionaries*, G5273.
3. Genesis 4:7

Chapter 22 – Spread the Peace

1. Luke 19:42

2. Galatians 2:20
3. Luke 8:23–25

Chapter 23 – Live Righteously

1. John 1:36
2. John 1:40-42
3. Mark 8:33
4. Luke 22:33
5. Luke 22:34
6. John 21:3
7. John 21:15-18
8. Matthew 16:17-19
9. Acts 3
10. Acts 4:1-22
11. Acts 4:23-31
12. Acts 5:20
13. Acts 5:29
14. John 21:15-19
15. Matthew 5:12